BEATING THE ODDS!

STORIES OF TRUTH AND JUSTICE FROM AN OLYMPIAN AND WORLD RECORD HOLDER

BY

PHIL SHINNICK

WORLD
ATHLETICS

Phil SHINNICK
USA

WORLD RECORD
HOLDER
Long Jump
8.33
Modesto, USA
25 May 1963

Dedication

I dedicate this book to all those in the world who suffer injustice and struggle against it as a way of life. This book is dedicated to those people who are in pain and suffering in sports by their own choice and who have not brought this on themselves but were forced by outside forces or accidents. They have the insight to heal themselves, figure it out, and not give up. There is a way out of this, and it can be found with patience and perseverance.

To the great thousands of year-old history of Olympians competing in peace during times of war, showing the world athletes can be brothers and sisters across national boundaries. To those who try to be the best in athletics, seek out the people who have the same heart and unify in peaceful competition through the love of sport and athletics.

Acknowledgments

I acknowledge all the athletes and my scientific and artistic brothers and sisters who shared their stories of truth and justice with me and supported me:

Muhammad Ali, Arthur Ash, Jesse Owens, Donna de Varona, Novak Djokovic, Simon Freed, Rafer Johnson, Leonard Bernstein, Roberta Flack, Boyd Gaines, Dr. Elana Pechdacova, Tracy Sundlun, Dr. Jack Scott, Gary Power, George Sauer, Lee Evans, Tommie Smith, Ron Davis, Guy Benjamin, Doug Harris, Dave Meggyesy, Michael James, Lacey O'Neal, Russ Hodge, Barbara Horne, Guy Obolensky, Dr. Rustum Roy, Dr. Effie Chow, Dr. Kevin Chen, John Thomas, Larry Tann, Dr. B. J. Cling, Kent Shinnick, Shannon Shinnick, Quincey Shinnick, Nelson Shinnick, Lew Hoyt, Laurence Porter, David Fisher, Mark Sendoff, Alex Hartnett, Dr. Yoshiaki Omura, Grant Birkinshaw, Susan West. He Bin Wei, General Mu, Maud Russel, Laurence Porter, Chloe Porter, Phil Clark S. J., Gordon Toner, S. J., Robert Goebels, Dr. Celia Rosenbaum, Marlon Raichel, Dr. Bill Tiller, Roger Guettinger (read and commented on the manuscript), Stephen Spahn, Blake Spahn, Kirk Spahn, Rick Mesmer, Lakshmi Ramachandran, Eddie Purovic, Monappa Hegda MD, and Jamie Taicher.

Table of Contents

Introduction

As a young man, in 1963, I competed in the California Relays at Modesto, my first big meet as a sophomore at the University of Washington. I beat the Olympic champion and world record holder, Ralph Boston, in the long jump to set a new world record and was voted the "Best Athlete," among four other world records broken that night before a packed stadium.

I was never honored for that achievement and discredited. The world record was never submitted. I jumped on the 1964 and 1968 Olympic teams and became captain of the 1969 US national team in Asia. I fought for 58 years to get it accepted. Finally, I was given an opportunity by Sebastian Coe, head of world athletics, who sent it to the Court of Arbitration of Sport. This was the spring of 2020, and that fall, the skin over my whole body broke out in a rash from anxiety.

That fall, I woke up one morning with a story in my head and immediately got up and wrote what was on my mind every morning for 33 days. I had a story in my head every day I woke up, and these are the stories in the order of those days. This is a creative endeavor and does not explain the years of struggle that went into finally getting heard in the spring of 2021. I was officially given the world record in a ceremony at the University of Oregon Stadium in the fall of 2021. The time was right!

KOMO TV in Seattle interviewed me, and I received an Emmy for the interview and was awarded Edward R. Murrey's Top Sports Story in 2021. I also got a very fine plaque, and other sports articles detailed the long struggle I underwent. This is not about that process but what came to my mind from waiting to see if I would be successful in getting the world record I deserved. Something I never got over until the plaque was in my hand.

Chapter 1: The Worst Day

I woke up not knowing where I was, disoriented, confused, pitch dark, no light, just a crack near a floor-length curtain. On the far side of the large room. *Where am I?*

I slowly put my feet on the floor, seemingly trembling like a rough sea, but I was weak-legged. I then stumbled, weaving side to side, focusing on the far-off streaking light. Pulled the curtain chord, opened the wall curtain, and started to faint. I dropped to one knee and then recovered a little.

The stark realization overwhelmed me! Finally, I had my first big track meet after two years of no competition; freshmen could not compete. Now, I am a sophomore at the University of Washington, just turned 20, on a track scholarship. I finally got to where I wanted to go. To me, this was a big time at Cal Berkeley against all the best collegiates on the West Coast.

To get here, I survived a head-on car accident at 60 MPH and hurled through the windshield (punched out with my right hand, which still hurts each day).

Three months after this near-fatal head-on at the Lewis and Clark Prom in Spokane, I switched from Washington State University on a track and basketball scholarship to track only two days before fall enrollment in 1961. My hand was no good for basketball; Jack Mooberry, the WSU track coach, never forgave me and harassed me during dual meets.

"We would win too if we had athletes in five events."

I answered, "Who do you have that can do five events and beat me in any event?"

He recruited me very aggressively while at Gonzaga Prep.

I played football for the first time at Gonzaga, which takes football seriously from grade school up. I grew from 5′ 6″ as a freshman to 6′ 3″ as a senior. So, football was out for me until I grew into my senior year.

Teammates in practice and other athletes in games went after me to hurt me, resentful that in the first game, I blocked a touchdown pass, tackled a half back behind the line of scrimmage, and caught a long pass in one quarter at a merry-go-round. I was punished for this. I was kneed in the ribs in a game, had my feet ripped from underneath me when I jumped high for a pass on defense in practice, and went head-first onto my head.

I couldn't remember where I was; the coach came screaming toward me at Gonzaga Prep and yelled, "I do not want anyone to say I cannot remember."

My right end position was no longer in the line-up; I stood on the sidelines wondering where I was. Coach Frazier then stuck his head under my chin guard and said, "Get him out of here."

My eyes were glassy, and I did not know who he was. But where should I go?

Phil Clark, my Jesuit scholastic math teacher, coach for all sports, and spiritual advisor, pointed to a building far off. I walked to that corner but did not recognize anything. I stood on its edge and wondered what I was supposed to do. Behind me was a door; I opened it and walked down the hall with a clickily clack, cleats on and in full uniform. At the end was the lunchroom.

Spokane 1961. Car totaled in the head in a car accident at the senior prom for Lewis and Clark High School

I then circled back and looked through a porthole. I saw a locker room. I entered and sat on a bench. I managed to take my practice jersey off. Looked at my shoulder pads and could not figure out how to untie the string. My dad took me to the emergency room, and I was out for one week with a brain concussion.

Earlier, in my freshman year at Gonzaga Prep (5' 5", 105 pounds), I was the starting point guard on the basketball team. I had broken all records in the high jump in the Grade School Junior Olympics, so I was a proven jumper. I did double pumps and was a flashy guard. I liked to fake a shot, then scoop it up on the way down or do a floater.

The coach said, "We do not need you to be fancy; you jump high and at the top of your leap shot."

My heels hurt for two years from coming down from so high, and I could hardly walk. It was a long way down. My shoes had no cushions or canvas keds. X-rays showed my growth plates had been crushed in both heels. I was out of sport for two years. I had special inserts. I took the bus downtown to Whirlpool therapy. Finally, after I got my growth in my junior year, I turned out for the basketball team. I had not touched a basketball for two years. I grew to 6' 2" and was put at center/forward. I could outrun and outjump anyone. I was the only athlete in the city to dunk and put on a show in warmups before big crowds and one-handed, two-handed, under, and over dunks. I could not dribble; the ground was not where it was supposed to be.

Shooting was difficult under the basket. I could still shoot from outside, but I was told to stay under the basket for rebounds. My competition was Dave Ferrier, 6' 8", and All-City. I replaced him in four weeks since he was slow, and I was the fastest runner on the team. The team could then fast break.

He got very mad, and when they put him in at halftime, after starting me, he scored 29 points. I could handle the ball, so I assisted all the shooters at high post. The first team was all shooters and didn't throw the ball at each other. So, we on the second team beat the first in practice and finally replaced the first team All-City forward and center.

In the spring, I did track and won the state championship in the long jump at 23', the same as my senior year, and my city record in the high jump and near city record in both hurdles.

After sitting out for a week in football after being knocked silly onto my head in practice, teammates jumped on me when I was on the ground, stepped on my hand so I could hardly use it, and sprained my ankle by piling on. So, I was a mess, but all the city athletes were watching me. I then became a decoy, going long, and then the quarterback passed short. I returned all the punts and couldn't be stopped, so I ran by defenders.

I healed during my senior year basketball season and felt liberated. Our games brought 5,000 fans to the Coliseum with triple headers. I went to dances both nights, getting home at 2 AM and then up for practice at 8 on Sunday. I was tired all the time and had a constant sore throat. A tumor started to grow under my chin, and it was removed. The biopsy showed a "giant follicular lymphoma, cervical node."

Doctors said I did not have long to live; this was terminal, so I might as well play basketball. In practice, I ran through the plays, did a head fake, and tore open the stitches. They stitched me up again that night and said, "This will hold, we put in 8 stitches."

After the next game, I removed the bandage, and four of the 8 stitches came out. I felt like I was dragging a sled while running, and at the foul line, I almost fainted several times but made the shots. I could still run fast and rebound. I had a hard time catching my breath, but I fought under the basket with taller centers who elbowed me. Finally, the season ended, and I stayed home for six weeks. I did nothing but rest. I recovered. Slept for 10 days, then slowly got better:

2/14/1961. Cancer Registry, Sacred Heart Hospital, pathologist report for biopsy of cervical lymph node: Giant Follicular Lymphoma. S-61-953. Condition on discharge. Alive. Curran Higgin, MD

In religion class at Gonzaga Prep, they said if you French kissed a girl, it was a sin. I went to Mass almost every day during the school year and wanted to become a Saint, so I switched girlfriends often to avoid becoming too involved. Also, I did not like confessing what I was doing. I do not think my girlfriend, Sandra Etter, was too happy with my other girl dates.

When we went out as sophomores, she was bigger than me, and I appreciated that she would even go out with me, but I grew, and we went to the senior prom together as king and queen. French kissing was a mortal sin, and you could go to hell for it. I did not want to get married or get her pregnant. Yet, she was my first love, and it remained constant during my high school and subsequent years—extremely attracted to her.

Summers in high school, I bucked hay bales on Charlie Miller and his younger brother, Jim's 20,000-acre cattle ranch in Sprague, Washington, 30 miles from Spokane. Charlie was just 21, and Jim was younger. Their father had a heart attack and died, and the grandfather was too old to run the ranch. I got 3 cents a bale, and I make $20 a day if I put up 2,000 bales a day with two other hayseeds, Gonzaga football players I recruited.

Each bale had to be handled three times: putting it on the truck, throwing it onto the stack, and then staking it. We started early in the morning and worked till 6 PM. We set a pace that no buckers on the neighboring ranches could equal, so I got lots of work on other farms. Each bale was 45 pounds with twine string; you picked it up; then, with your knee, you bucked it onto the transports.

Later in the summer, I could pick up two bales in each hand, drop them by the trailer, and then buck up four bales. I put a tractor in low gear to run by itself and then would run up and put it in neutral while I bucked the bales onto the trailer. My other hayseeds, Gonzaga friends, hustled to keep up.

Back in Berkeley!

The morning of the 1963 Berkeley conference championships, I stumbled to the window and pulled open the curtain. I recovered and came to my senses. Today was the day I had been waiting for, all those hours on the farm bucking bales and my two months walking and hitching with a backpack through Europe with my friend Paul Swift sleeping in the open fields; I wanted to become a Jesuit. Paul Swift did join the Jesuits in a year. His father had the city record in the long jump in 1929, which I broke, and elder Swift broke the national record in the 220 at 21.3. Paul Junior was a good sprinter in high school. I wanted to break records in high school and at college, which I dreamed about almost every day.

1959 and 1929 Paul Swift Junior and Senior

Paul Junior asked me to meet his father. When I got to his house, Paul Sr. had a pipe in his teeth. He looked at me and said this is how you do it. He lay on the floor and said jump on my stomach hard, which I did. As I did, he had a fierce look on his face and a deep smile while tensing his muscles. His eyes were bugging with deviance. I jumped up and down on his stomach, and he did not move or flinch. He said this is how you do it. I got it. Be a tiger!

Later, I found he was right. The abdomen is everything, so each day, I jumped up and hung from the goalpost while raising my feet to my hands 3 x 20, then did three sets of 25 in a pike position, laying on my back on the grass, feet, and hands touching.

So, now was my chance to show what I could do. I was at the Durant Hotel in Berkeley (1963), and the stadium was across the street; the long jump was at 9 AM that morning. I had butterflies and weak knees. I got dressed to prepare for my big chance. I walked into the next room, still agitated. Brian Sternberg, in his shorts still in bed, seemed not up, so I threw a newspaper, in my hand, at him, and he leaped out of bed, swatted the paper, and gave me a menacing stare. He got dressed, and we went to breakfast; it was not yet 7 AM. The stadium made me uneasy; at Gonzaga Prep, they showed pictures of the free speech movement and the demonstrations. I felt a ghost of this agitation. I did a long warmup, ran through my steps, and put a small piece of paper in the long jump pit at 26'.

In previous weeks, I defeated Mel Renfro (who jumped 26' as runner-up at the NCAA championships in 1962 for Oregon) in the rain against the wind at 25' 2" and the next week did 25' 7" at Pullman in a crosswind. Renfro seemed to falter in both meets, not getting near 24'.

Berkeley has cold mornings, and this was no exception. The wind swirled through a tunnel on the west side of the stadium. My first jump was just short of the 26' mark, but I fouled by a fraction. My next jump was closer to the paper mark, but also a foul. I knew that I could now get over 26'. I moved my steps back four inches. I was one of the top college jumpers in the US and undefeated.

I went past the 26' paper mark in the pit, and the jump was fair (I did not go over the take-off board). I was so happy; I ran around like a chicken with its head cut off, yelling and jumping up and down. The official stared at me and then raised the red flag for a foul jump. I went to the board and put my spikes in my spike impression on the board; it was clearly a fair jump. He said I did not have my balance. I do not think he liked my show of excitement and being three feet better than the next jump; he was suspicious of the jump.

There was no rule about not having your balance, only not going over the take-off board and exiting the pit by not going backward. I ran to my coach, and he examined the spike marks and agreed.

He took me aside and said, "Phil, no jumper is over 24', so you are two feet ahead of anyone. Do this: run down the left side of the runway, and I will put a piece of tape there behind the board. Just make the finals."

In the NCAA, you get four jumps before the finals. I did this and hit the mark several feet behind the front board and had a perfect landing, a great effort, but when my heels hit, it was hardpan, the pit had not been raked there, and I skid on my back, and where my head hit, it was 21' 5 ½". I missed the finals by 1 inch; I was out of competition.

Brian struggled in the pole vault and, the year before, was the national freshman champion. He mastered the fiberglass pole. He was a star trampolinist in gymnastics. Never really trained in track; he would come out and do several wind sprints carrying his pole but never came to track practice, just worked out with the gymnastic coach on the trampoline.

1963 UW Husky Stadium. Sophomores Phil Shinnick, Stan Hiserman, and Brian Sternberg. Shinnick jumping in UW Stadium

Brian was fearless; from the UW pavilion, he walked over to the Montlake Bridge (barefoot in his brief swimming suit) over the canal between Lake Union and Lake Washington and stood on the rail. It must have been 8 stories down. He said he wanted to perfect a triple somersault and double twist. He did the jump perfectly. The motorist must have thought he was attempting suicide; probably, for most, it would have been their end.

I entered the high jump at Berkeley. I have no memory of jumping. No one wanted to hear what happened; when I started to talk, I could see no interest, so I stopped. Lew Hoyt, who became the NCAA champion in the high jump from USC, was on the grass next to me and saw my remorse and utter disgust with the injustice. He asked what was wrong, and I told him the story, and he believed me. We became best friends, and I later coached him in Athens for the CISM military championships when he was faltering.

I could hardly talk, and Lew just sat next to me, saying nothing but staying with me. He won easily. I couldn't eat and was comatose; this was the worst day of my life.

In 1961, in February of my senior year, during the period I stayed home from school after the diagnosis of cancer, I slept for ten days, ate a lot, and watched some TV. Then, I slowly started to get my strength back and realized what caused this illness.

The beatings I received in football, staying out too late during basketball season, and kissing too many girls while never resting after my throat hurt. I wrote away and got the films of all the great high jumpers, long jumpers, and hurdlers in the world. These were stop actions with frames from the beginning and end of each event. I went over each frame day after day to get an idea of good form. In the high jump my sophomore year, I was city champ with my brother Nelson, but I jumped on my side, the Western roll getting up to 6'. John Thomas and Charlie Dumas jumped over 7' with the staddle.

So, I wanted to switch and watch the stop action of the straddle form. In my first meeting after my illness, I set the city record at 6' 3" with the straddle form. I did not practice the straddle. I only had proper form in my mind, and in each movement in the jump, I tried to copy the Russian Brumel and American Thomas.

Left. 1955, 12 years old (4' 9"), and 1966, 23 years old (7' 1/2").
Both records. Western and Straddle technique in high jump

But I had many days and weeks at home, so I turned to my grandfather, Doc Shinnick, a surgeon from Idaho who had a set of encyclopedias and a complete volume of Greek and classic literature. So, I spent my time reading Aeschylus, Sophocles, Euripides, and Aristophanes about Zeus, Apollo, Achilles, and Ajax. I found Ajax interesting, and the messenger who warned that Ajax was:

"Doomed to meet Athen's wrath,

"'For, said the prophet,

"'The gods have dreadful penalties in store,

"'For worthless and redundant creatures,

"'Mortals, who break the bounds of mortal modesty.'

"And Ajax showed he had no self-control,

"The day he left home,

"'Son,' said his father,

"And very properly, 'Go out to win,

"But win with God beside you.'

"'Oh,' said Ajax,

"With vain bravado, 'Any fool can win,

"'With God beside him, I intend to win,

"'Glory and honor on my own account.'"

This was Ajax's first fault, but after Achilles' death by Apollo, his shield was given by Agamemnon to Odysseus, not Ajax, who showed honor in battle but not given to him, leading to Ajax's madness and suicide. I saw this as a warning to seek glory and honor for myself and not to go mad if earned yet ignored. In many ways, this was a warning and a prophecy.

Chapter 2: Driving to the Meet, Cowboy on a Ranch and Horseback Riding, Summer Hitchhiking in Europe, Running with the Bulls in Pamplona

At the Berkeley stadium, I sat all afternoon and could not get over what had happened to me. A fair jump disqualified me? I conjectured it might be because other jumpers, on this windy, cold morning, could barely get over 23'. Some jumped under 22'. What to believe? I felt the official made up "not having your balance."

Even if off balance, how did I get past the 26' white paper in the pit? I broke the sand past the mark and exited the pit behind the break in the sand. The mark was a small white flag sticking up two inches above the sand; later, they outlawed this.

On my second jump at the 1961 Washington State high school championships in Pullman, I cleared 24' and had a new state record. A foot and one half better than the next jumper. The official brought me over to the wood 8" board and put my spikes into my spike holes.

Clearly, I did not go over the board. He took a square and put it on the ground so that the angle was 90 degrees up. He was on his stomach and gladly announced I was one degree off, yet my toe did not go over the wooden take-off board. Later rules required putty on the front of the board so that the toe would make an indentation. The toe had to go over the board by an inch for there to be an indentation. I got robbed. I became the champion at 23' 1" but did not have the State record.

At Berkeley at about 5 PM that day, May 25th, 1963, as the high jumpers finished (I could not make 6' 8"). My head was not in the high jump. An official came up to me, still sitting next to Lew Hoyt, who was jumping well.

He said, "Phil, we would like you to come to Modesto for the California Relays. Ralph Boston is there, and we know what happened here."

Sternberg made 15' 9" and was sloppy; he won, but he could not believe how poorly he performed. He wanted 16'. So, Brian and I got into the back seat of a car. We still had our ankles taped, and I still had sand in my crotch.

After each jump, my shoes would fill up with sand, and it went into my mouth many times when I landed with my head down from the splat. As we went over the Berkeley hills and into the valley going east and south, I could feel the warmth of the valley. Was this a reprieve? The air had velvet thickness, and our silence became animated. John Pennel, a world record holder with the new fiberglass pole, would be at the meet. Boston was an Olympic champion and broke the world record several times; he would be there. He was the first man over 27'. My legs seemed to come alive.

In 1961, after my senior year, Charlie Miller made me the foreman of the ranch so he could go on vacation after we put the hay up. I helped his neighbor do the same. Going across the ranch took half an hour to get to a far field (20,000 acres). When he got back from vacation, he asked me if I could ride a horse. Yes! Old man Dix, a polo player who lived on the next block, brought his horses up from Hangman Creek behind his house in the alley. I was so happy when I could run and put my hands on the rump of the horse and vault up.

For $1.25 an hour near the polo ground off Hangman Creek, we kids would rent horses and wade the horses across the creek and up onto the bluff two blocks from my house on the south side of Spokane. We ran the horse across trails and downhill all out. To make money for horseback riding, In the summer, I had up to 5 lawn jobs for $5 a week and mowed lawns for $1.25.

In the winter, I shoveled snow for driveways and worked with the family coal shovel, which was heavy but could scoop lots of snow in its belly. It was heavy, but I got used to it and could shovel a driveway in half an hour and make $1.25. I chopped wood for an old lady before school and, for a free lunch, cleared the lunch tables, swept the gym floor, and then ran out to play baseball on the playground during the noon hour.

So, Charlie Miller had me drive his truck to an open field while he and his ranch friends went out on horseback to bring in a horse for me. After waiting for some time by the gate, which they asked me to close, I saw a great white stallion run out of the woods with the ranchers herding it. He was surrounded by the horsemen and was one angry horse.

All year, it had been in the pasture with his mares. It was only ridden in a roundup. They herded it into the corner of the fence, and they trapped it. Everyone got off their horses; we made a semicircle with barbed wire to the side behind the stallion. He was up on his back legs angrily snorting at us with front paws menacingly, quick front leg strikes on two back legs.

Charlie turned to me and said watch this. He had a blanket and was saddled next to him. He picked them up, walked right up to the stallion, and put them down, the stallion raising up again and again on its back legs. The stallion snorted and warned not to get close. Charles walked right up to him, still up on his two legs. The stallion came down on all fours, and Charlie put his arm over his shoulders; the horse stood still and swished his tail.

He threw a blanket over his back, put a bridle on him, and saddled him. Clenched him up, told me to come there, and said, "Here is your horse."

With leather reins in my hand, I walked the horse past the open gate. The other ranchers were on the other side of the gate and smiling at me, which meant I might be in trouble.

See what the greenhorn can do, I thought.

I vaulted up on him without putting my foot in the stirrup in one motion. He started to buck. I turned him around, kicked him on both sides, took off to the near hill at full gallop, and raced him uphill.

At the top, he was so winded he could hardly breathe, so I waited, and when he got his breath, I raced him downhill at full speed back to the ranchers on horseback. He veered to the left, and I saw some trees ahead. I knew what he was up to; based on my Hangman Creek rides, he was going to take me out with a low branch. He ran with his head higher as we approached the tree, and then, just before we went under the tree, he lowered his head.

Meanwhile, I was nearly out of the saddle with my head under his neck. When we cleared the branch, he turned his head and looked at me. Not yet convinced he couldn't buck me off, I raced to the other horses and stopped. The other horses were snorting, ready to go, and the ranchers started shouting, "Let's go."

He bucked once more, and I held onto the saddle horn; the other horses took off, and he, like a kid near a playground, then ran after them.

It took the better part of two days to round up all the cattle in separate fields and bring them together. We rode 18 hours a day, stopping at 3 AM and up at 5. The second night, near pitch dark, we had all the cattle into one small field, and two bulls started fighting since all the cows were together, and the smell drove them crazy.

They ran at each other and head-butted, and with heads together, they ran sideways and hit the barbed wire fence with steel poles holding it up. The steel stakes went down hard; the fence was on the ground. I got the signal we had to go across the downed barbed wire and get the bulls and cows that followed them back. It was messy! The horses and bulls and cows got their ankles ripped up.

16

I got to the bunk house late and went to bed; I felt something in my sheets and jumped out. They were mice! The hayseed friends I recruited put mice in my bed and were hysterical with laughter. I was in no mood for these tricks (they had been doing similar things all summer). I put the light on between the bunk beds, saw the mice, and wanted to kill these hayseeds. The other hayseed was in the upper bunk above me. I knew the danger of my mood, so I lifted the hayseeds' double bunk up and flipped it over with him inside.

His eyes were like he saw a ghost; he was frightened by my strength and kicked me as hard as he could to my right shoulder. I knew if I hit him, he would not live, so I looked at the light bulb, squeezed it with my hand, and watched the effervescent shattered as the tungsten wire now in the air lit the space around and went out. I went back to bed, and it took me some time before my breathing became normal. My shoulder was damaged, but I ignored it. It became a problem later in my jumping career.

Charlie got me out of bed while it was still dark, and we started to herd the 3 or 4 hundred head of cattle to Sprague thirty miles away. By the third day, we all took our saddles off and rode bareback; everyone had their six guns in their holsters, except me, the greenhorn. I had no gun. The herd moved slowly toward Sprague. A bull took off running for the woods a quarter mile away. My stallion, without my urging, took off, running as fast as he could to cut off the bull.

Once in the thickets, the bull would be hard to get out. It was an all-out race; the bull was moving at top speed, and my horse raced straight at the bull. I felt the power of his all-out gallop. He did not waver.

Just before the crash, the bull stopped on a dime, looked at the horse, turned around, and walked slowly to the herd. As he got closer and smelled the cows, he took off running and stuck his nose in the source of this fragrance or freedom, a dilemma. We made it to Sprague and the railroad yard. I jumped off my stallion and went over to the creek, put some water over my head, and stood up. Charlie Miller came behind me and threw me into the cold creek.

Everyone else was on their horse, shot their six guns in the air, and laughed hysterically. Charlie got the greenhorn. I was fully soaked, and Charlie was laughing so hard he could hardly run away from me. They shouted, "Charlie, he is after you, so watch out."

I ran him down, tackled him, and dragged him by his ankle to the creek. "Charlie was a great football player," said those people who used helmets were sissies. They played 8-man football in this small town. I picked him up and threw him in; he was over 200 pounds but seemed light. The guns went off.

"Hey Charlie, who got who?" And almost fell off their horses laughing and threw me a quart of whisky. After a long swig, I threw the bottle to the next guy.

In 1962, in Pamplona, Spain, after my freshman year a year earlier, Paul Swift and I waited for the bell to go off at 7 AM so the gate would open and the bulls and cows would run to the stadium for bullfights at the fiesta of San Fermin. We were at the gate as it swung open.

All the other red-scarfed, all-white-clothed runners were up the hill around the corner, waiting for the running of the bulls. Fearing them but wanting the red scarf, which signified they ran with the bulls. When the gate swung open, we saw the bulls were only interested in the cows, so there was no movement to go out of the pen.

Someone inside shooed the cows out of the corral toward us, and the bulls followed. The cows liked getting out of the corral, so they took off in a trot. We were not five feet away. Paul Swift, my summer hitchhiking partner, and I were both runners, so we wanted a fair race. We would try to get to the stadium before the cows and bulls. The bulls were bred to never see humans, as told to us by Arther Greenfield, who wrote *Anatomy of a Bullfight*.

Along with 5 others, they drove from Paris together to Pamplona for the running of the bulls. We had been in Paris drinking wine and singing international solidarity songs; two young novitiates climbed the seminary fence to be with us. Others were socialists, and some spoke only French. Paul was better than me at it, but I could understand the drift of the conversations.

We gathered at Jay Ross' apartment (sports writer for the *New York Herald Tribune*) to eat his chicken and red wine stew. He put my picture on the front page of the 1963 May 26th issue of the Paris Herald from my Modesto jump. It said that I was a summer Paris resident.

Each night, these two seminarian students climbed the fence and met us on the Ile de la Cite. Swift and I swam the Seine after diving in from the island. We all drove down to Pamplona for the Feast of San Fermin for the running of the bulls. Swift and I then hitchhiked down to Madrid and then to Lisbon.

Driving south into the valley after the terrible 1963 conference meet in Modesto, I felt euphoric; there was justice in the world. I was given another chance.

Years later, in 1969, in Moscow, jumping against the great Soviet leaper Igor Ter-Ovanesyan and former long jump world record holder, the newspaper called me the "Great White Horse." They maintained that the only reason that the American athletes could beat Soviet athletes was because of the Black athletes, namely Ralph Boston and John Thomas. In Moscow, I was greeted with a star-like status that I did not have in the US. Here was a world-class White athlete like them, the Great White Horse.

In the back seat of the car driving, Brian sat next to me in full competitive uniform, and he was feeling the same reprieve. Even though the day was waning, our bodies started to relax and get energized. It seemed to get warmer. Berkeley was an ordeal; the ghost of the free speech demonstrators, the swirling wind, and the chilly morning all gave me the most miserable day of my young life. The day was still early, and I was eager to change it.

1962. Above Paul Swift Phil Shinnick, three female students and two male seminarian students in Paris

To the left. Phil Shinnick, Jay Ross (sports editor at New York Herald Tribune) and Paul Swift in Paris

Chapter 3: Driving to the Big Meet, Leaping Off Sand Dunes and Steep Roofs, First Competition in Portland Indoors

My first (of my career) was a big indoor meet in Portland, Oregon, and I traveled with my UW track team by station wagon to the Glass Palace. Coach Hiserman entered me in three events: the long jump, the high jump, and the high hurdles. I was becoming a very good high hurdler and challenged Mike Thrall, nip and tuck, our star hurdler indoors in the Hec Edmundson Pavilion, which had a 220-dirt track indoors where we ran short 60-yard hurdles races out of starting blocks and a gun.

Portland had a plywood board track, which was bouncy and fast. The first event was the heat of the high hurdles, Ralph Boston, CK Yang, Mel Renfro, and Jerry Tar (Renfro and Tarr near the world record). I was so happy to be given a chance, and here I was; my warmups were good, happy, and ready.

The gun went off, and I got out fast; I was over the first hurdler quickly and kept form, but where were the other hurdlers? I could not see anyone in my peripheral vision. Had I falsely started? I hesitated and got third in my six-person heat by a chest length. I made the finals. What was happening?

These were the best in the world, and where were they? The finals came, and Thrall and I made the finals, so this was familiar. I got out fast again, and the same thing happened. I could not see anyone up to the fourth hurdle. Where were they?

Thinking during a race slows you down, and I ended up sixth; all the runners were lunging for the tape feet apart, including me. Even at sixth, I had one of the fastest times in America. This was exciting. I measured my steps in the long jump. There was Ralph Boston, who did well in the high hurdles and beat me by a hair.

Running down the runway, which was much faster than the dirt runway in the UW Pavilion. I felt the same power I felt hurdling. In my turn-up, I raced down the run and felt like riding my white horse. I was way over the board and ran through the pit.

Next jump, I adjusted my steps and tried again with the same feeling, and way off the take-off board, I ran through. My third jump felt the same, and even with the adjustment, I was off. Three fouls with run-through and no jumps; I was out of competition, but I still had the high jump. I made 6' 6" easily and thought, here I can do well; in the field were 7' high jumpers from Oregon. The world record was near that.

On my 6' 8" jump, I came in easy and planted with great authority, vaulted over my take-off foot, and could hear the plywood ricochet. The standards for the crossbar shook, and the bar fell off before I could spring over it. This happened three times, and I was out of competition. I was raw power, and the fast plywood threw me off balance as if on a trampoline, shaking loose the crossbar, which fell off.

Ralph Boston was watching me. He was a great hurdler, high jumper, and world record holder in the long jump, first-person over 27'. I could see his steady glances.

Still, I felt happy; I just needed to race the high hurdles again and not be shocked to challenge world-class hurdlers, run with eyes straight ahead, and pay no attention to my competition. But what happened to me? I was different, with great competition at another level of speed and power. In the long jump, my new speed meant a different length on the run-up. Dirt was different from wood, which was much faster.

After two hurdle races, three attempted long jumps, and great effort in the high jump, my legs had a new challenge. They were twitching and felt a deep ache. I opened the station wagon door and sat in the front seat, which had legroom.

A 5' 6" upper-class distance runner tapped me on the shoulder and said, "You go to the back; this is for upperclassmen."

I looked in the back seat, which was taken, so they opened the back door of the wagon. I got in the jump seat, my legs were on my chest, and I was facing backward. It was a three-hour drive to Seattle. When we got there, I could not straighten my legs.

"Prometheus Unbound,

"From my sickness reading refrain,

"… let the lightning be launched with curled,

"And forked flame on my head,

"Let the air confounded,

"Shutter with thunderous peals and convulsion of raging winds,

"… with the stars eclipsed in their orbs,

"Let the whirling blasts of necessity,

"Seize on my body and hurl it,

"Down to the darkness of Tartarus,

"Yet, all he shall not destroy me."

I felt I had to go deeper inside myself to overcome this injustice of selflessness by a teammate in my fateful car ride; this could not destroy my career. Yet, my leg would not be released after two months. I went high up into the stands of the pavilion and put my right leg out on the plank seats. I stretched my hamstring.

It would not give in to relaxation; I had gone too long in the knee-on-chest position for three hours after my Portland indoor meet. I decided I would not move until it let go. I would burn in hell before I would give up. I breathed and confronted the hamstring. I waited 5 minutes, 10 minutes, 20 minutes. I was not giving up on this tension after 40 minutes, and I would have waited an eternity. I heard a screeching sound, not tearing, but the muscles letting go, and the sheathing of the muscle had stuck together and moved. The hamstring let go, and the noise of sheathing becoming smooth continued bit by bit, and in 10 more minutes, it opened.

I had to do the same with the left hamstring, which was about the length of time. I was liberated. The next meet was in Eugene, Oregon, and Mel Renfro, the top long jumper in the US the year before, was there. Bowerman elevated the long jump runway, which was plywood, very fast. It was raining, and the wind was blowing in my face. I stayed in form, did not run all out as before Indoors, and jumped 25' 2". Renfro could not get over 24'. I think Bowerman knew he had a problem on his hands with me. Next week in crosswinds and cold in Pullman I jumped 25' 7" at the NW Champion Meet, Oregon, Oregon State, Washington, and WSU.

The tension that Brian and I felt that morning in Modesto seemed to be a harbinger of what was to come that morning. He could hardly pole vault and had his worst meet for over a year. He was a freshman national record holder at 15' 9", and here he was just matching his freshman mark.

We started to chat; we warmed up to each other. His new girlfriend occupied his mind; he had been awkward socially, but now, he was becoming famous. I was bitter about the morning, and my feeling of injustice started to pass. The warm valley silk air seemed to get in my body, even though I had been competing since 7:30 AM, starting my warmup and high jumping all afternoon. We had not eaten all day. The valley was a wonder to me; I saw farms, cows, horses, and open fields. I felt at home!

Brian and I gravitated to each other emotionally; we both wanted to break all records, world record breakers Boston and Pennell, at the meet. Wow! Just what we wanted, we both wanted to challenge the best our hearts desire. This is what we lived for; I felt I was an heir to Apollo, Achilles, and all the ancient Olympians. It was in my blood, in my soul, my heart, and my body. This is who

I was; only a person like Brian understood. He was the same; he had mastery of his body and could flip himself in the air and control his space. He was the trampoline national champion.

Above 1944 Nelson, John and Phil Nelson Wilma and Phil

Dad asked Edwin Nelson if he could marry my mother, and he said, "You don't have a pot to piss in."

So, Dad waited by the side of the road as Wilma drove to Boise for Edwin's inauguration as a governor. Old Ed was heartbroken since she was only 17, Dad was only 19, and just a year of college and no money to go back. Dad waited on tables at the inauguration while his brothers and sisters had guest seats. He was serious about making money for his newlywed wife.

Then, Dad accepted a construction job in Midway Island in the South Pacific while Wilma rented a house in Grangeville, Idaho. Midway was bombed by the Japanese while he was on the island, then came back to the US and joined the Army and went to officers training school. The war ended before he got out. The local paper showed Wilma up on the porch repairing the roof, which women never did.

In the winter, to get firewood, she went to the woodshed where rats lived and had to beat them out with a shovel to get wood.

Mice ran around in the walls, and a rat got in the house, and she caught one up on my bed while I was asleep. She then went to live with her father several blocks away.

1956

This was the day I had been waiting for ever since as an eighth grader at Jefferson Grade School on the south side of Spokane. My best friend Ann Gillis was in my art class, and Mr. Hovis, the art teacher, was taking us to Hangman Creek to make masks with plaster of Paris on the sandy shore of Hangman Creek. It is a steep drop to the creek where Chief Spokane had his tent.

Young kids would throw rocks at his tent. He had a ranch in the valley but went on a hunting expedition in the Selkirk mountains, and when he got back, an immigrant homesteader took his ranch and told him to leave by gunpoint.

Indians had no rights in court. He moved his tent to Indian Canyon (after being harassed at Hangman Creek), where I played golf with Ann, who became the Ohio amateur golf champion and later voted the best art teacher in the US. We had a contest to design the graduation announcement, and I won, but she was ecstatic that I won, and of course, she got second. She helped me carve in rubber my design for our grade school.

I wanted to impress my classmates, so when we got to an open field before the great sand domes, I took off running as fast as I could. Ann, who was also my ski partner, could not keep up. The rest were way back.

In my mind, I remember how I would run off the edge of the great cliff domes in the summer and land on the soft sand on my back and then slide in the sand to the bottom, which was about equivalent to a 50-story building almost straight down. I wanted to impress. I ran off the edge, flew many feet, and dropped straight down.

When I landed on my back, I hit a hard pan (it was spring). It jolted me and bruised me up with scratches. I knew that if I skid down, my skin would be taken off. I would be out of control. I stood up, slid a little, then looked down to the bottom and saw rocks greeting me and fifteen feet of sand after and before the creek.

So, I started to flip in somersaults, in arches; this was easy, and I timed the arches to land in front of the rocks and then leap over onto the sand. It worked! I turned to see if the other students were at the top, and I heard, "Is he dead?"

They were standing at the top, peering over like birds on a telephone line. I knew Brian, an athlete of my kind, would have figured this out as well.

This idea came to me in a similar situation when I was ten years old. I hit a ball up on a roof that was stuck on the roof of a two-story house four houses down from my house on Sherman Street in Spokane. I do not remember how I got up to the apex of the rooftop, but it seemed too dangerous to go that route down.

On one side was a dormer, and the other just a steep slope. Accidentally, I started to slide down the steep slope. I could not stop the slide standing up. Looking at the gutter, I thought if sitting down, I could grab it as I flew off. This seemed risky! I looked out on the lawn and decided to run off the roof and jump onto the lawn. This I did, and after landing with forward momentum, I somersaulted three times, stopped near the sidewall, and then walked home. Vera Bilkowski knocked on our door and told my mother I jumped off the roof and was now alright.

My mother turned to me and said, "Did you jump off the roof?"

I nodded and said I was fine.

After my scary somersault down the giant sand dome, I was all scratched up and had some bruises from landing on the hard pan in the spring. I remembered I had a softball game at Comstock

Park and had to go home to get my bike to ride to the park, but I had to run up the bluff on the south hill to my home to get my bike. Then I rode four miles, which tired me out even more.

As I arrived late, the Wilson opposing coach said, "Shinnick, go home." Just joking!

Wilson Grade School had fully matured athletes in eighth grade. I was 5' 4" and about 98 pounds, but a good athlete, the Wilson coach, came up to me after his insult and said to me, "If anyone hits a home run against my team, I will give them the bat and ball of the game."

I was very tricky with the pitches, like I was with Michael James later in Nicaragua, so they could not hit much. My turn up to bat, they had this big bruiser pitcher, and he had a sidearm that seemed lightning fast. I crouched low and kept my eye on the ball in his hand. He did his warmup and threw it hard, like a snake striking; I sprang up with my legs, uncorked my body, and hit it squarely. It flew over the left fielder's head, and I practically walked home; I got the ball and bat, and the Wilson coach was all smiles.

Chapter 4: Arriving in the Night to the Big Meet, The Sun and The Moon Kissed Each Other, The Great World Record Leap

Brian sat on my left side in the back on our car trip to Modesto for the California Relays; we both had our all-white competitive uniform on, with purple stripes of Washington across our chests. Silk all-white briefs. Ankles taped had not eaten all day except for our quick sunrise breakfast.

The antagonism and both of our complaining of the morning and afternoon ordeal were starting to fade a little. Brian never seemed to fit into the track team; he rarely came out to practice, did his pole vaulting at odd hours, and spent his time on the trampoline.

The team had to go through daily wind sprints and timed 220s or 330s on our cinder track, which was soggy from the constant rain. A really hard workout to practice on the track. Brian never did track workouts. Brian came from a religious family and was not social with my teammates, was a bit awkward, and did not talk small talk.

His national record as a freshman put him in a higher class than me since I did not have meets my freshman year. The fiberglass pole just came into our sport several years ago; he had done well with the steel pole because of his strength and mastered the fiberglass pole in short order.

He was invited to regional and national meets during his freshman year. The world record had just gone past 16', and he had done 15' 9" the year before. He was sloppy that morning, missed easy heights that were low, and barely won the competition—the worst performance of his life.

We knew one had to perform at the right time in competition to get a record. We both wanted to make history. I could perform under pressure with no practice in most field events. If I got a picture in my mind of the proper form, I could coordinate my body to fit into that form under pressure and at the right time in the high jump, long jump, and high and low hurdles. I was a fast sprinter, but few could do the jumps, so I was not allowed to sprint because, in high school, you were limited to three events.

Doing five events later in my senior college career week over week weakened me for the nationals at season end. This year, because of my frozen hamstring for four months, doing daily stretching, whirlpool, and a trainer digging into my hamstrings daily in great pain had no effect.

So, I was limited to just the long jump or sometimes the high jump. I had never been in a position to be overshadowed by a teammate. Brian was a level above our track team; I was untested. That day in the grandstands changed all that. My hamstrings had been released after all these months. I did not give in to this injury.

To get records and be honored, one had to be calm under pressure and not have a scattered mind; this required long hours of mental rehearsal, going bit by bit over the form and seeing oneself in action while not there. I secretly did daily prayers and, in the early mornings, snuck out of my Sigma Nu fraternity to go to Mass at Sacred Heart, about a mile away. I thought if I told of my religious practices, they would mean nothing. Then, I would be doing these to be praised for being religious.

People had to not know humility in practice, which seemed to be the way to be a saint, to get to heaven, past the last judgment. So, how can one strive for honor in sport and not be egotistical and lose their soul? This was the challenge!

With Brian, I felt free to talk about my religious practices since that is where he came from. Earlier in our freshman year, we talked about religion openly. Things were different now; his social awkwardness meant he had no girlfriends or social life. Now, he was in love! My focus on honor and performance was a constant schism I tried to figure out.

Smiles came often as we looked out the window in the valley and awaited our newborn opportunity. Modesto was at the base of Yosemite with almond orchards. The officials of Modesto were farmers, had a love of sports, and did their jobs for no pay. Modesto was the best meet in the world.

Everyone would flock from all over the world just to be on the scene and compete with the best; no one got paid, and gold watches were given to the winner. A deep glee overcame us, and we stopped talking about his new girlfriend or my injustice. My high school illness made me reluctant to date, or I would be six feet under. I knew my vulnerability in kissing girls would be my demise spiritually and physically. I learned my lesson.

We both had the same idea: we were hungry. We asked the driver to stop for food before we drove to the meet when we approached Modesto. It had to be fast since the meet had started. We needed fast food, so we went for a drive-in and ordered a hamburger and milkshake. It was 7 PM. I don't think we swallowed the food.

At 7:05 PM, we arrived. We could hear the roar of the crowd; races were going on one after the other, and the Junior College State Championships were being held at the same time. The stands were packed, people were standing around everywhere; the air was electric. I saw all of the world's great athletes in person: Parry O Brian in the shot put, Al Orter in the discus, Bob Hayes in the sprints, John Pennell in the pole vault, and Hayes Jones in the hurdles, Peter Snell, Jim Beaty in the mile, many world record holders and Olympic champions. Too many to name.

I walked to the long jump pit and was told I was right before Ralph Boston; someone had heard about my jumping and gave me a good spot. I could not believe my good luck. It appeared I was getting a retrieval from injustice.

The lesser jumpers had already jumped, and there was a pause between the second to last heat and the elite heat. The pole vaulters were warming up. After measuring them, Brian and I helped each other with our steps and then ran down the runway to check.

Everything checked out after we both did run-throughs. Brian checked the board for me, and I looked at his take-off point while planting the pole. People were everywhere, and all the top officials were at the long jump, expecting Ralph Boston to take the world record away from Igor Ter-Ovanesyan, the Soviet world record holder at 27' 3 ¼".

I laid down on the grass, did some stretching, and looked up into the sky. What I saw was a revelation; instead of a blue sky that blanketed the atmosphere, I could see through the blue clear-up in the cosmos. Far off was the universe peeking through the veil of blue. Twilight time. Depth now came to my senses. I was euphoric; no religious exercise could match this.

As I stood up, I saw the Sun in the west starting to set over the grandstands, and to the east was a full moon. They were facing each other in all their glory, the silver of the Moon and gold of the Sun. Kissing, it seemed, each with an overwhelming presence. Frozen in their embrace. They called my name; I had warmed up on the runway. It was a black rubber-like substance and fast. A new composite runway. The board seemed very near; the end of the pit seemed short but was 30 feet. I felt this in high school and, on my city record, jumped over the 23' pit onto the grass. A longer pit would have given me more room in high school. It was 7:13 PM.

Running felt like I was on that great white horse; there was no effort on my part, and I felt for once uninhibited, no thinking, effortless. On the first jump, I went over the board by a hair. Boston came over to me as I exited the pit and said I jumped 26' 8", what Jesse Owens jumped for his world record, which stood for decades. So easy! Brian had seen the jump since he was watching my steps. Big smiles. We walked together back to the end of the runway.

"Brian, I am going to break the world record. If I do it, will you break the world record in the pole vault?"

I knew it would come on the next jump. We circled like gunfighters, eyeing each other. He raised his hand to me; I saw his bicep muscles bulge as he extended his hand. We shook.

"Let's check the wind."

He ripped off a small bunch of grass and threw it up in the air, and it fell to the ground. "Perfect conditions for a record."

My name was called again, and I walked to the end of the runway. The officials all had their eyes on me. I could see this as an exciting moment for them since Boston jumped the first jump near 27' and was on the verge of a new world record. A historical moment for the officials. I challenged myself.

It was now about 7:20 PM. A gun went off, and I looked across the field and saw the start of the junior college low hurdle race.

Should I go or wait? No, the time is right. I must go and ignore the race, I thought.

Again, I felt I was riding a power unbound and free. I looked over to Brian down by the take-off board, and he gave me a thumbs up. Again, tested the wind. I hit the board perfectly for a fair jump. I felt as if I pushed from behind and became airborne, and my hips went above those around me. Icarus in flight! The landing was off-balanced, the pit was 30', and it appeared I would hit the cement at the end. The measurement was 27' 9" on my right foot and 27' 5" on my left, not a good landing. I could hear the crowd roar as they saw me airborne, and still, there was an unsettling in the crowd, sort of a gasping.

Brian was at the take-off board, watching to see if my spiked shoe had gone over the toeboard. When I landed, and the first measurement came in, we hugged, reaping with excitement and joy. He knew what he had to do—27' 5", a new world record.

The San Francisco Chronicle recorded the first measurement, but after multiple measurements after the sand caved, the jump became 27' 4". May 26th, 1963

Old hawk-eye, as Boston was called, was right there in the pit and said he would check the wind. He walked just feet up the runway where the wind gauge was stationed for both the sprint races and the long jump. Just 8 feet of grass separated the runway to the finish line for the races, which was at the pit, came back and said the wind was ok for the low hurdle race.

To get a world record, it needs to be measured by independent officials. Many officials wanted to do the measurement, to say they measured a world record after the third measurement (putting a pencil through the hook at the end of the steel tape measure and placing it in the firm sand). I watched the sand cave bit by bit as each new official, one after another, jumped into my footprints. Repeated measurements collapsed the sand back to

34

27' 4", still a world record. I yelled stop; it was caving in. They did. They could not believe it and tugged the steel tape measure hard, pulling the edges of the sand to cave in from the pencil into the imprint.

Still, the meet and roars went up in the crowd for other marks, the discus, javelin, and shot put. By the end of the meet, five world records were broken, and performance at all levels went to new marks. In the mile, Peter Snell put on a sprinting kick in the last 220 and went past Jim Beaty, American record holder in the mile. Snell missed another world record by .1 seconds.

The announcer could not find my name on his program, so he first announced that my hurdle teammate Mike Thrall, who missed his hurdle race, had entered the long jump. A page from the newspaper section high in the stands said I was needed in the stands.

Still with sand in my shoes, I walked up the cement stairs, which were very difficult with spikes on. I thought of stepping up backward. As I got high up, a reporter shouted, "Who are you?"

I felt offended to have to shout my name, so I retorted, "Who are You?"

Someone else said, "That is Shinnick."

Going down in spikes was more difficult since I had long spikes on to get leverage and stability on the wood board. This was a big chore. I still had four jumps left since this put me in the finals; I was irked. Why didn't they come down to the pit and ask their question? I was not some errand boy.

I prepared for my next jump, but nothing changed. I still felt like a racing horse, and things felt easy. I had gotten a fair jump, my run-up was solid, and I was confident. I felt I could jump onto the cement 30' out, and this did not scare me. I had done it on grass in high school, and at worst, I would get a little scraped up. I felt the lift on take-off.

Instead of propelling up, I spun in the air, landing backward in the pit at about 25' but facing the runway. My shoe had split, going up those steps weakened by the take-off shoe. It came completely off my foot and was up on my ankle. That was it! I did not have another shoe.

Unlike later long jump shoes, which had a built-up platform and were reinforced around the side, this was a six-spike sprint shoe, which was good for my hurdling, which I had not done since the fall season. It was all over for me. I felt I could have gone further, but still a world record. How unhappy could I be?

Brian was next up. I helped him with his steps before, and he started at a higher level than usual. Since we got there late, he was on the last flight next to Pennel, American record holder, while inching up the world record. Brian broke the world record at 16' 7".

So, he made good on his promise; we were two happy dudes—both 20 and hardly started our college careers. Comparing all the marks that day to other meets and the Olympics, by far, this was the best track meet in history. I was voted the "Outstanding Athlete of the Meet." A clock on a wooden pedestal and a little bronzed runner, they had quickly carved my name on the plaque. I got what I wanted all these years on the farm, every day attempting to surpass the number of bales bucked, averaging 8,000 lifts a day in the hot summer sun on the sage of Eastern Washington. The summer before my two-month trek through Europe on foot, with a pack, while hitchhiking (auto stop), sleeping out in open fields with the cows built up my legs.

Chapter 5: Two World Records, Celebration in the Moonlight, A Long Retreat in China

Brian and I could not eat after the meet; we had that hamburger and milkshake just before I jumped, and ripping my shoe made it possible to stay near Brian, who was faultless up to the world record height at 16' 7". John Pennel had already missed and was out. Brian soared over the bar with room to spare, and I think too excited to go beyond that. He was fluid in motion, and his gymnastic acrobatic ability showed.

When the pole went into the box, which created a shock on the pole and a warp, Brian's strength in his arms by pressing the pole so it would bend his way, tilted backward, and was upside down with feet in the air before the pole unraveled and threw him sky high over the bar effortlessly.

The stiff steel pole required even more strength, and our other pole vaulter, John Cramer, was much better at it because he was even stronger than Brian but did not have the gymnastic flexibility. He had to switch over, had not mastered it, and had a higher height on the steel pole than Brian. Still, he was high up in the competition.

Getting the most valuable athlete among many world record breakers and gold medalists seemed to erase disappointment from my demise for a further distance after my ripped shoe. I harbored resentment of those sports writers who put me in the position to rip my take-off shoe. No one walks on cement with spikes on; one walks on their heels, but going upstairs is different. I could not walk uphill on my heels. Why didn't they come down to talk with me?

Then, shouting at me, "Who are you?"

I was insulted. This passed.

It was late when Brian finished, jumping in the dark. The stands were full, and all the competitors stayed around for the finish of other events. Another world record? Someone else coming out of the woodwork? A dizzy night, and human performance was unparalleled. Everyone wanted to be a part of these historic moments. Fan or athlete. It seemed that our energy was still on the rise as midnight approached.

Still, with our ankles tapped and full competitive Washington uniform on, we drifted out of our motel room and walked into the orchard. The silver Moon lit the orchard, and we could see almost across the field. We walked far into the orchard.

Brian then jumped up, grabbed a branch, catapulted up onto the limb, and sat there looking at me. As a boy, I did the same over the fence on Sherman Street in Spokane. The neighbor had high bars 20 feet up with swings, and I would shimmy up and hang upside down by my heels. My mother was terrified, but my dad taught me how to do it, and he showed me how. This scared me as well, so I practiced on low bars and then, with courage, did it on the high bar.

"A.E. Housman's *Ode to an Athlete Dying Young*, early though the glory glows (men and boys stood shoulder high), it wilts quicker than a rose." I quoted something like that—not accurate, but close—to Brian.

"Phil, we just set world records, and here you are throwing water on it."

"Look at this Moon, which cast shadows before our feet. Isn't this pure beauty of power? What have we done to match this? Honor is not immortal, but we can be immortal if we protect our souls."

"Forget it! I have my world record and a beautiful girlfriend; this is enough for me right now. Why are you talking like this?"

"I am being cautious. Haven't you heard of the last judgment? Everything you did will come before judgment day, and a world record may not mean much if you wander from goodness."

Brian somehow jumped up on the branch again, then jumped off, and, on the way down, grabbed another branch, swung high, and landed perfectly on the ground. He looked at me in disgust while gazing at the shadows of the Moon and the thick plasma of the air. He took a deep breath, flipped himself in the air, leaped up, and sat on the branch. I was not sure what to do, so I just jumped into the dirt. We smiled at each other; I was finally Brian's equal in honor.

"We compete for honor but need to renounce it. When I jump or you vault, we cannot think of honor or records, or we will not be able to be free and let things go without thought of the results."

"I miss Nancy, and for now, I do not want to think about anything but enjoy what I have: a world record and a loving girlfriend. What more could a person have in this life? Why can't we just stay with this? We are young!"

We both lifted our arms to the Moon, which seemed to cover the sky, breathed in the fragrance of the orchard, went back to our trees, sat there for hours, and watched the Earth rotate as the Moon chased the Sun from east to west.

Finally, the Moon waned, and the Sun's streak came over the orchard waxing. The Moon had been our calming friend and companion, shining on us as I raced like a great horse. Brian bent the pole and vaulted up, not touching the bar.

1990

In Qigong, the first principle is to put your mind in the lower part of your body. For two weeks, in the morning, afternoon, and evening, our group focused on the lower part of our bodies. My scholar friend, Dr. Kevin Chen, and Bin Hui He, the abbot of one of the Taoist temples in Lao Fu, organized a tour through the temples of China ending in Lao Fu, where Bodhidharma reached enlightenment.

Bin Hui He was a traditional Chinese opera singer and national weightlifter, and Dr. Chen was a co-author of many scientific works. These two weeks were a build-up for the Lunar Moon. We were together in a small room while young Chinese therapists worked on our feet and legs.

Bin Hui He turned to me and asked, "So, what happened at the ceremony?"

Kevin translated.

I waited in perfect tranquility on a wooden bench outside the ceremonial room residing in my third eye from my Siddha yoga daily practices. A thought came into my mind. You must embrace the silver moon and its yin energy.

Breaking my meditation, I looked up and realized why China is called Zhongguo or center Earth. The Moon was in the center of the sky itself, covering a third of the sky and casting a canopy over the whole Earth to all sides of the curvature. I remember that night at Modesto. I closed my eyes and embraced this silver energy, exiting my third eye, and could feel my whole body as I felt something happening on the top of my head as if being touched, then slowly like the Moon in the sky, in all directions, poured down slowly on all sides until I was full of silver moon energy.

I thought this was great, became giddy, and smiled. *It was time to go into the ceremonial room for the moon initiation by Abbot He*, I thought. I found the furthest part of the room so as not to be noticed by Abbott He, and then skipped the ceremony and continued to soak up this plasma-filled feeling. Abbot He went to me first in my corner and tapped on the top of my head, initiating me in the Chinese Lunar Moon ceremony.

Immediately, I felt the tap on the top of my head, and a greater force entered my body. I was in a half-lotus position on a cushion. I raised up about eight inches on my hunches and came down, uncontrolled; it came faster and faster as if riding a horse.

Pretty soon, I wondered, *How could I be going up and down so fast? And how much faster could I go?* It didn't stop. I thought I better lie down, a little scared. Fully stretched out, my whole body shook for about half an hour. This ceremony happens once a year, at exactly midnight.

After the ceremony, I meditated all night at Lao Fu under the Taoist temples till sunrise. I remember that night at Modesto, where Brian and I did the same.

Abbot He listened intensely to me with Master Chen, then gave a big smile, did a thumbs up, and said, "You got it."

The next morning after the 1963 Modesto jump, before our flight back, the Modesto officials gathered and voted to support my jump as a legal world record long jump. I arrived back at my Sigma Nu fraternity, and on the sidewalk in red was a 4" wide line of 27' 4" with increments for each foot.

I walked into the house, and someone said, "Hey, Phil, too bad you did not get the world record."

I was shocked by the comment. I found out that the wind gauge official had not recorded the wind measurement. Later, I found newspapers around the world reporting it as a world record, but on the West Coast, this became the refrain. I felt like an arrow had been shot into my heart from this comment. But I had three more meets till the end of the season.

In two weeks, I went to Compton on a cold night with a cement-like runway and new shoes that were too big, and I had to put cotton on my toes. There was a crosswind, and Ralph jumped 25' 7", and I jumped 25'6 ½". Brian rebroke his world record. It felt good to be in competition with Boston.

Chapter 6: Brian is Paralyzed, Brian Stars and Shines, Wind, and Officials Torment Me

Depending upon what people read or heard by the grapevine, responses to my jump went from disbelief, adulation, and respect (from athletes) to tough luck. Your jump did not count, and better luck next time. Here, a jump is defined by the media or popular misconception.

In the rest of the world, the official error was not reported and put on newsreels as a new world record. No official at the meet denied me the jump and voted to submit it as a world record. I think people like a good, hard-luck story in which one can do spectator things but can be taken away in an instant.

This resonated with many: "I would have been good, but I got an injury and therefore could not do sport again."

It encouraged me that Boston and I were jumping about the same given conditions at Compton or the Coliseum Relays. Having him beat me just by a fraction was heartwarming for me. We were at the same level. I was picked up in a private airplane in the Bay Area to get to the meet, with a pilot and Rafer Johnson, the Olympic gold medal in the Decathlon, and myself in a small three-seater.

Johnson jumped 25' 6" in the long jump and threw the javelin way over 200'. I competed against CK Yang, who got the silver medal in Rome; in the pole vault, he flirted with the world record at Portland. Two of the greatest track athletes in the world had a close friendship. We talked non-stop the whole several-hour flight outside of LA. He wanted to know all about that day at Berkeley and Modesto.

The next big meet was in Albuquerque, New Mexico, next week for the NCAA National Championship and another chance to compete against the collegians. Boston was much older. Brian again showed his prowess and won the NCAA championships in the pole vault. The runway was fast, and I could see that the anticipation of competing against me heightened the field. My steps were on, and I felt good.

In my first jump, I tested my steps by running pretty slow, learning my lesson at Berkeley, and making the finals. I jumped near 26' easily and relaxed. The other jumpers were below me, and I felt confident about another attempt at the world record and winning the meet. My shoes fit! Within minutes, the wind picked up, and these young jumpers started recording spectacular leaps, way over 26'. First one, then another until I was in sixth place. I felt happy and ready to go.

I looked at the end of the pit, which looked short, taking off, feeling that same natural sense of riding a horse, trying to maintain balance. A great leap, people gasped after I landed in the pit; it appeared to be nearly 28'. The red flag went up, and I went to the board and saw my toe went over by a fraction. The wind was stiff, and I was not happy since it would be a wind-aided jump and not a world record.

Still, I wanted to show my stuff! I adjusted my steps and moved them back by six inches just to make sure. Again, it was a great leap, in control and below my top speed, to get a good flight in the air. But the day was over; the finals would be the next day. All those above me had wind-aided jumps and were not legal, but in competition, these counted for jumping orders for awards.

The next day, I could hardly wait; I just needed to get a fair jump. I warmed up, and the weather was warm, but they changed the direction of the pit, and the wind was gusting and constantly in my face. Not good for a world record!

The officials came over to me and said, "You had world record jumps yesterday, but we could not certify for a world record even if you didn't foul because of the wind, so we switched the runway to the opposite direction. Good luck, and let's get a record."

In my run-through, I had to move my steps up because of the resistance of the wind. Going down the runway felt like I was pulling a sled, yet I was strong and felt I could get a good jump. I had done this before in Oregon against a wind with rain. My leaps were in the mid 25'. I had the best jump of the day. Other jumpers could not get over 25'. However, I jumped over 25'.

I won the day, but the previous jumps, which were wind-aided, counted for placement. It was over; I did not win nor get a good jump. Brian was happy being the national champion, and I was not as remorseful as in Berkeley since at least I got a jump that was fair but not good enough to place high.

Brian and I stayed together and went to St. Louis for the US Open championships. Boston would be there, as would Darrel Horn, an Oregon State jumper who had done well. This meet determined if you got on the national team for the Pan American Games, but I did not know how that worked or where these Games were.

We were greeted as stars, went to the race track, and met all the important, famous, and rich people in Missouri. I loved horse races; in Spokane, I would go to the racetrack often and get next to the dirt track to watch the horses close up.

In St. Louis, Brian and I were ushered into the owner's circle after the important races. I went over to these magnificent horses, chest-butted them, and leaned my body against them. They liked this and would turn their head around to look at me, and I would bang their honchos with my elbow. A friendly howdy du. The jockeys looked at me with big smiles and did the same. Horses are very physical in this way.

The weather conditions were hot, hot, hot, and I wanted revenge to prove myself as not a flash in the pan. The long jump was scheduled for 6:30 PM, and I was ready to go.

When the time came, my coach came over and said, "They have delayed the event by 10 minutes, so stay warm and do some easy wind sprints. I cannot go into this affair too much; it is still too painful."

This went on for an hour. Hiserman, my coach, told me the same: "Keep warm."

Finally, at 7:40 PM, they started the event. All the cameras were stationed at the end of the pit, and the crowd was ready for a world record attempt. I ran down the runway pretty fast and jumped the 24' 8" just to get a fair jump. Yet, my take-off leg did not feel strong. I increased my speed and hit the board perfectly, but my leg collapsed. This happened again, and I got 8th place.

By my calculation, I did about 100 wind sprints from 6:15 to 7:45 in 95-degree temperatures and humidity. I was not used to this heat; I did not mind the heat, but the humidity was near 90%. In the hay field, it got up to 95 degrees all day, but dry heat and humidity drained my strength.

I could sense what had happened. I was now ignored as a flash in the pan. Brian then became the sole hero, the NCAA champion. AAU champion and world record holder.

Next to him, I was like a porter holding his bag. But he still was my buddy and understood what had happened. He was named "North American Athlete of the Year" and "The Most Decorated Athlete" in 1963. We flew back to Seattle, and he was the talk of the town; people did not know what to do with me except to be silent around me. A world record breaker who could not win in big meets. That feeling I had after Berkeley then became constant. How could this happen?

Tom Toomey, the Dominican priest with whom I had become friends, heard my sorrows and reminded me what the difference was between climbing a high mountain and jumping; he did not get it since he was not an athlete.

"Put it in perspective," he said.

How could I?

This did not console me, and except for Brian, who had been around the pit helping and watching me, <u>no one</u> knew the real story. The season was over for me, and Brian was named for a meet against the Soviets and other big meets. I was off the national team, but one of the best jumpers in the world. Yet unproven! My sleep was disturbed, and now I had to wait a year for another try.

Brian was back with his girlfriend, so we did not talk much except for him to say the world was his, and he glowed with the thought of a good girlfriend, fame, and good health. Why worry about immortality or his soul? He had it and would be in the record books.

As for me, my mistrust of fame now tested me. At the deepest level, I wanted to be the best in the world and put my name on records. So, was it a contradiction to talk about my soul like I had been about my soul when I really cared about being a great athlete like Rafer Johnson?

Nevertheless, I was invited to a special meeting in Eugene against Ralph Boston next week, where just the two of us and some others would match off. I think Bowerman sensed how good I was and knew that I was inexperienced and would do well in my career. He saw me in action in Eugene, Pullman, and Modesto.

Brian did not want to leave his girlfriend; his future was secure for international competition. He and I felt we both would up our world records, but now, he wanted to win against foreigners, and this Eugene meet meant nothing. For me, it meant another chance to redeem myself against Boston. I was not worried about how I would do it; I knew the Oregon runway, and there was no pressure, just Boston and me.

The car ride for me had anticipation in it, but also, the deep injustice of what had happened sort of split up. In St. Louis, they postponed the competition because they felt it was too hot to get a record but did not tell me the delay would be over an hour (running on the field for immediate competition, which did not come) in New Mexico, the officials wanted a world record but how could I do that against a wind?

Over the radio, a news flash came: "Brian Sternberg had been paralyzed from the neck down by a trampoline accident when he was attempting a triple somersault and double twist." This was exactly what he told me later. I do not remember anything about the Eugene meet, as I had to get back to Seattle!

Chapter 7: Brian Is Dropped on His Head, Therapy Is Going Bad, Retreat to Alaska

The University of Washington Medical Center took charge of his care. I entered his room, and he was in bed. He was not happy to see me and was in great pain.

"What happened?"

"They put screws in the side of my skull, spread-eagled, stretched out, suspended, and rotated every few hours on a huge machine. This went on night and day. In the middle of the night, the cable broke, and I went down about five feet onto the hard floor on my head and stayed there for some time, unable to move. Getting me out of that contraption was painful; if I did not get paralyzed from the trampoline, then this did the job."

We just sat looking at each other; more than anyone knew what he had accomplished in the cold at Compton, breaking the record in less-than-perfect conditions, and he understood correctly what happened to me.

In breaking the record at Compton, he understood that going all out was not the way to a record in the pole vault. The pole did most of it, but it bent differently under hot, cold, dry, or damp weather.

Staying in form and dealing with the conditions meant records for him. There are no foul jumps in the pole vault, only if the pole goes under the standards and the bar gets knocked off. In the long jump, they measure at the end of the board. Up to the 1964 Olympic trials, I had 7 world record jumps just over the board.

At these great attempts, the run is different, and if it is off by 2 inches, then it is a foul. So, in the trails, I jumped off the runway, 9" behind the board. Huge, foul jumps do not count, and I made the team with 26′ 3 1/2″, but not 27′ jumps; better safe than sorry. Yet, measuring from my take-off, I was jumping 27′.

We talked about what they were doing to him.

I came back every day. This day, he was in a small pool of water about 4′ deep with three aids around him, getting him to move his arms and legs. He was in great pain and said, "Get me out of here."

He was mad! I told Brian you need to do this if you are to recover. He looked at me. He never swore and said, "Fuck off, I know my way; God has done this so that I can be a testament to His grace."

Each day I visited, our conversation was always centered around eternal grace, pain, and recovery. I felt my career was over, and I lost all desire to try again to redeem myself. I felt rudderless. Father Tom Toomey, my close priest friend, saw this. I came over to the Newman Catholic Center one early summer day, and he handed me a plane ticket.

He said they were building a church in the woods in Soldotna, Alaska, on the Kenai peninsula just southwest of Anchorage. I was to stay with a church woman in Anchorage and then go to Soldotna. I hitchhiked down the peninsula over protests by the worried church women after one night.

"Just wait a few days for a ride. It is not safe."

I thought, *Who could hurt me?* So, I left the next morning with a small bag.

Jim Romanski, a Portland volunteer, and I shared double bunks in a cabin, so the small two could not stand up. At night, if a mosquito got into the cabin, its buzz woke us up, and we had no choice but to turn on the light to kill it. They were as big as bees and gave a nasty bite. Working at the church required a sweatshirt with a hood, a beard, gloves, and not letting ankles exposed. They were relentless, always buzzing around my head.

Father Ameroult, the priest, got Weyerhaeuser to donate stacks of 4" x 4" wood. These were stacked on top of each other and secured by bolts. The first roof was blown off, so it was replaced, but they forgot to leave air in the crawl space. Without this, it would rot, so it needed to be ventilated.

My job was to drill holes 18 inches from the ground through the 4"x 4"s all around the church. I had a drill and bit, the old-fashioned type; the holes needed to be close to the ground opposite the crawl space. I could not rotate the handle around as it hit the ground, so I had to go back and forth, and the bit did not go through the wood without hard force. I had to dig my toes in, flat on my stomach, usually in the rainy mud, since it rained a lot. A messy, hard job, and the mosquitos never went away. This took weeks.

We walked up the dirt road to a cabin to get breakfast. No one had money, but we had flour and butter, biscuits, butter, and jam—lots of them. Sometimes, we got salmon for dinner, and when we had no food, our priest would take us to the only diner near us, and we could order anything we wanted. He had no money and wondered how he would pay. He toured the tables with his priest collar on, making friends and always laughing. He was very personal and really loved the lumberjacks, who were big and tough. He mentioned me and my record, and they stared at me, so I waved.

Eventually, someone would say, "Let me pay your bill." He winked at us, and boy, that meal was good since we had gone weeks without a good meal. Flour, butter, jam, and occasional salmon were not so bad.

1963 Soldotna Alaska. Jim Romanski and the family that fed us, the father worked in the Salmon Canning factory, and the nephew on the right helped us with the church. The wife cooked for us.

The brightest thing that happened was one day, we were building a walkway from the rector's house to the church. When it thaws out, the ground gets sticky with thick mud. The thick forest surrounded the church and rectory; on one side was the dirt road to Soldotna, and thick trees were all around.

Out of this forest, which we did not venture into, came a girl, about 20, my age, with red hair and a radiance of energy I had not seen in the lower forty. I was on top of the walkway building the roof, so I jumped off, landing 20' off. Brian would have been proud of my dismount.

She came to see me and was attending Sunday mass with her parents. She saw me, but I never noticed her. I had been deep in prayer. We went into the church, and I showed her the floor I had built in the sacristy. Then, we drifted into the main church, we walked closer and closer together, and then we were in an embrace that seemed to last forever. I felt her vibration, and it was different from anything before; she had been living in the woods, had a natural glow, and was uncorrupted. Her face was pure!

She said, "Why don't you visit me?"

We walked outside, and she pointed out where she came out of the woods.

"Just enter there and go until you see my house. It is not far."

Every day, I thought of entering the forest to see her, but I also knew that one can get lost. Also, I had my duty at the church. Day after day went by, and I did not enter the woods but thought about it.

To this day, it still enters my mind that here was a woman, unscathed, uncorrupted, a natural beauty, and someone to be true to. It had been a year since my journey through Europe. My love in high school, Sandra Etter, had a suitor who came to her house every day for years, and I was 300 miles away from school. I had asked her to our big fraternity dance my freshman year. But I was in Europe between my freshman and sophomore years. Todd Hullin, a fraternity brother, said I should ask Dana Hall from Queen Ann High School for a dollar party.

Immediately, I was enticed by her, and we seemed natural together, dancing, holding hands, and laughing. I took her home and was overwhelmed. She asked me inside, so we kissed and hugged and knew that we had something special, giddy and happy. I noticed a glow in the dark from the hallway; it was a lit cigarette. Her mother was at the kitchen table watching us.

I talked with her later in the week and asked her out again. She told me that her mother objected to me and told her she could do better. My girlfriends' mothers always loved me since I respected their daughters, was tall, and had a good presence, so this hurt me. I stopped dating and continued my quest to become a great athlete.

Several years later, I ran into her mother in the great quad on campus. She was taking a class, and her older son, Cam, was the student body president. She apologized and said she made a mistake. I called Dana, and she picked me up in a car, and we parked. I thought she was the one! Each day during that year, I thought of her. I just wanted to ask one question, and we would be together.

"Do you believe in God?"

She equivocated, stuttered, and talked about God being all present but would not say what I wanted her to say. I opened my passenger door and started to leave. She asked me to stay so that we could work this out. I said I just cannot be with a person who does not believe in God. I left! That moment still haunts me. She was right and more advanced than me in understanding the universe.

Thirty years later, at an intensive Siddha yoga conference, I was assigned a seat in a big auditorium. It was next to Tom Toomey, my old Dominican friend who sent me to Alaska and was now the chaplain of this giant 3,000-person ashram. We went to the cafeteria, and Dana Hall was in line. We both had a similar reaction. I later lost her phone number, and I had jotted it down in a book, but it disappeared.

This working Alaska retreat had the effect that Friar Toomey wanted; I stopped my remorse over Brian and decided what I needed to do was make the Olympic team and win the gold medal. Learn to get fair jumps.

This was the only thing that could overcome my public-perceived failure, for me to jump again a world record. There was a cloud over my world record, which I did not understand. This was more important, making the Olympic team than a world record. In many people's eyes, it is better than a world record, although in a century, 25 gold medalists, but a world record, only a handful.

I had no money, only a $75 postal money order from Paul Swift as reimbursement for half I spent bringing him to Europe on our hitchhiking odyssey. I decided to hitchhike down the Alcan highway alone to Seattle, 1700 miles. I had 1 dollar 75 cents and the postal money order. I knew I could fast if the situation called for it.

Chapter 8: Building a Church in Alaska, Adventures Down the Alcan Hitchhiking, Childhood Retreat into the Mountains, Racial Politics

Nighttime in the North is between 11:30 PM and 1:30 AM, so I had plenty of sunlight to make it down the Alcan. I just left; I didn't ask anyone. Even though I asked Romanski to come, he was told he had to put up the winter storm windows on the rectory before he left.

I told him it would take one day; he said, "They said three weeks."

They wanted him around, as he had been there for over a year. He just came for the summer. The road out to the highway took about thirty minutes of walking, so I was off on an adventure.

Earlier, Romanski, who later was killed in Vietnam as an aviation gunner, hitchhiked with me down to the spit off the end of the Kenai peninsula. Moose seemed to not like cars on the road and would not get off, so they ran ahead of the car until they got tired. No one cared!

We heard of the Salty Dog tavern at the end of the spit at Hope from some Irish masons who had built the chimney for the church. The story: one man decided to physically challenge this catskinner of a woman (caterpillar tractors are slow, noisy, and very strong), and she got him in a headlock and made him cry before she let go. I wanted to meet her.

We had to walk out to the end of the spit and bellied up to the bar. I didn't see her, so I looked around. Apparently, she pushed Romanski aside and faced me sort of menacingly. She might be thinking of having fun with me. I was ready!

I faced her square and said, "At 14, on my grandfather's farm in Idaho, I was a catskinner, pulling a disc behind the combine in the wheat fields; it was dirty and hot."

She turns to Romanski, who tries to be inconspicuous.

"Come on, boys, I will buy you a drink; let's go sit at that table."

All the lumberjacks and construction workers were staring at us.

She wanted to know about what caterpillar tractor I was driving, a "TD-9."

Yes, each day, I changed the oil, lubricated the joints, and wiped down the engine from the dust. My teeth were black with dust, and my overalls seemed to gather all the black dirt from the whole field.

"Tell me more!"

I told her I was not happy because I got so bored I lost concentration and took out a barbed wire fence post. I saw a badger coming across the field toward me, and I stopped the cat, jumped off, and charged the badger, thinking it was after me and my cat for disturbing its field. He got up on all fours, and we went at it, but I had a steel bar, and I killed it. I felt it was the worst thing I had done in my life, and I was truly sorry.

She understood! Then, I went on to talk about my world record and the disgrace it brought me. And Romanski and I were building a church, and I felt this was my repentance for the badger.

She waited some time, and the mood was sober. She got up, and the whole tavern gave a sigh of relief. No fight! We were okay. She walked away and then turned to us and spoke, "God bless you, hope to see you again, and share a beer."

She was big, I was 6' 4", and she was that but much bigger, nearly 250 pounds, but clearly a woman with big breasts. She had long hair and always had her hat on. They said someone challenged her while drunk, and she knocked them out with one blow. Everyone wanted to be on her good side. Several years later, during the Anchorage earthquake, the spit went underwater, so the tavern became a way for small fish to hide from the big fish.

Plenty of time to think of other things while hitchhiking. I reflected on the previous summer with Paul Swift, coming back to Paris after hitching through England, France, Spain, Switzerland, Italy, Germany, and now back home. It was about 3 AM, and luckily, we got a ride clear to Paris from Rouen off the Seine.

Suddenly, the police pulled us over and, with guns, told us to get out of the car. They went through our packs while radioing other police. Just tourists. What's up? Someone had attempted to assassinate Charles De Gaulle just ahead on the road.

The next morning, we went to the president's palace and saw the Citroën with hundreds of bullet holes in its side. 91aulle, his wife, the driver, and the car made it back to Paris. How? Everyone thought De Gaulle was a hero, unkillable. It was right-wing French nationalists angry at him because he, they thought, was too friendly with Algerian nationalists fighting for independence.

1963. I helped build the Catholic Church in Soldotna, Alaska. Phil Shinnick and Jim Romanski built a walkway between the rectory and the church.

The whole trip down the Alcan went smoothly; I did not have to wait days for a ride. One day, a carpenter in a port city in the Yukon picked me up and then veered off west. One had to go east from Anchorage, then north to Tote Junction, and then south down to the Yukon, Northwest Territory, and British Columbia to Seattle.

It was nearly midnight, so I walked into the woods to get some sleep before the sun came up several hours later. I knew insects do not like the movement of a stream, so I walked until I heard the sound of a stream. It was pitch dark, but the night sky gave some light. I saw a fallen tree, so I laid my sleeping bag down and put my back against the log.

The stars had my attention, clear and transfixing. I heard some pebbles from the stream bed crackle, stop, then start. An animal was coming up from the stream toward me. All my senses were on alert! I saw its shadow; it was a mountain lion. It stopped about fifteen feet away, then turned and looked my way. Its eyes glowed in the dark, and I waited. Should I get out of the sleeping bag or stay put? I'm in a cocoon in the bag and cannot move freely. *No. Do nothing.* We stared at each other. I was not afraid; I was only trying to figure out what to do, and he did the same.

The cougar did not move; over its head, I could see movement in the sky. The Aura Borealis pulsated in the sky above, and then, its plasmic arm reached down and hit the ground gently, not like lightning.

Then, it bounced off in the space between us, turning at a right angle back into the woods. The cougar and I were shocked and amazed. Its path into the woods was through an opening. Its multicolored plasmin streams left a trail of light still pulsating, its head racing through the forest—a dragon, now showing its rainbow body colors. The cougar watched it, turned to me, and then followed the dragon through the forest opening. I fell asleep. The cougar was friendly, just trying to figure out who I was and what I was doing in the forest. I was in its domain; it had been on its nightly territorial boundary routine, probably not that hungry. I was just a curiosity.

The next night, I decided not to sleep in the forest but to just walk all night, which was only about two hours. This was scary; the sky was cloudy, so there was no starlight, and I could not see even two inches ahead of my eyes. Each step I took made a crunching sound like the cougar made on rocks; I was telegraphing my presence to the forest animals each step. I would take a few steps and then listen, and I heard all sorts of noise on both sides of the highway. Why did they put gravel down on this section?

Usually, it is just dirt and dust. I noticed the wind was blowing in my face slightly so animals ahead would not smell me; behind my fragrance left a ghost-like scent. I decided not to turn around. What could I see anyway? I would hear anything on the road behind me. What was out there? Certainly, something on both sides.

When my brother Nelson was 14 and I was 12, I took my grandfather's pickup truck near Riggins in the Selkirk Mountains in Idaho after meeting with the Rangers (my grandfather had been the head of the Idaho Fish and Game Department).

After many hours up narrow, steep mountain dirt roads, we arrived in a high meadow. My brother was an Eagle Scout, and my grandfather trusted us; you could drive at 14 in Idaho. We had our 22 rifles, pellet pump pistol flour, potatoes, and other provisions, but we were counting on the fish we would catch to eat. We could not catch any fish; then, my brother and I figured it out.

The fish felt the vibration of the banks when walking near the creek and our shadows. The creek was three feet deep and three feet across. We crawled on our bellies and then carefully dropped a hook baited with a worm over the bank, and boom, rainbow trout for breakfast.

On the second day, Nelson decided to follow the creek, which turned into a stream as more creeks joined and would follow it downhill, dropping sharply. I was to stay up in the meadow until he returned near our campsite and pickup. I watched him descend, and then, out of sight, I turned back to the meadow and walked across it.

In the middle, I stopped and felt I was being watched. This feeling of being watched on the Alcan by animals was not new; the only solution was to sit with my back against a tree and stay still. This was safe, and this is how I figured out that the log at my back would overcome any fear.

Also, all animals are not there to eat you; just trying to figure out what this new smell is. Walking on this Alcan road scared me, but knowing wild thoughts and fear creeping into my head, they do no good! Just hold on; keep moving. Each step made noises for everyone to hear. My back was not against a tree but open and pitch black.

I had made up my mind that I would become a Jesuit; my friend Paul had already signed up. Yet, I had unfinished business with sports. I devised a plan! I felt that my mind was all conditioned from my early life; my fears, anxieties, and whole personality were nothing more than my conditioning. Where was I?

Going back to Seattle, I practiced doing the opposite of my desires or thoughts arising. Already, I had done this with sex, girls, and kissing. I would expand this to all things. Back in Seattle, if I walked to school a certain route, I would every day go another way. If Friday night I went to a show, I would stay home; going out to dinner, Saturday I would stay home. But I could not tell anyone what I was doing as this was my meditation.

Also, I woke up at 6:30 AM to attend mass; all my Sigma Nu fraternity brothers slept in on weekends, and I would do the opposite. The biggest challenge was going to the dentist and getting Novocaine. I would get my teeth filled without it. I thought about it and then devised a scheme; when I heard the sound of the drill, instead of being tense, I would totally relax. Whenever the drill went into my teeth, I would watch my breath, and it seemed that all my senses went forward. So, I would go backward in the chair and sink into it, collapsing. It worked, and I felt no pain!

Harriet Beal, a UW student officer, spoke to me about redlining in Black districts in Seattle; blacks could not get loans outside the red area. I talked with Brian about this, and we decided to do something about it. This was called "open housing," and we would give a press conference. The other undergraduate with the same star status was Carol Peterson, the head majorette for the Husky marching band and National Baton champion (Seafair Queen, from Queen Anne Hill). Beal talked with her, and the three of us did this. I then went to downtown Seattle and handed out leaflets for open housing by myself on a street corner.

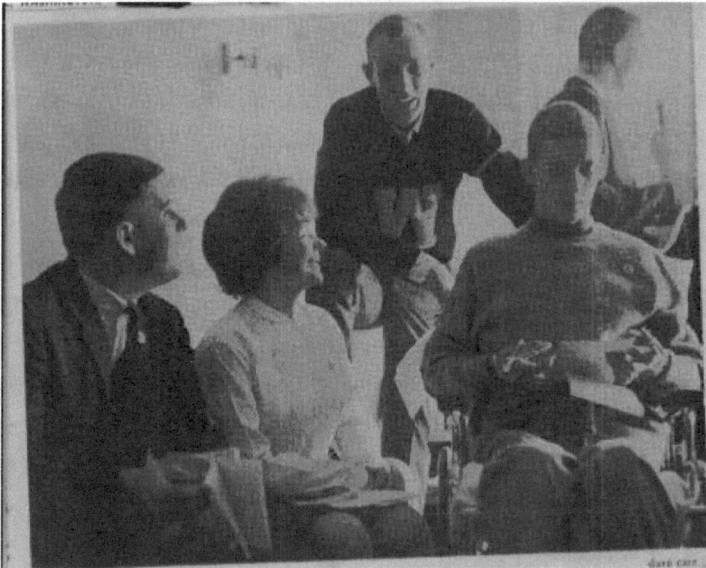

David York and Harriet Beal UW student officers Phil Shinnick and Brian Sternberg with buttons, "I Believe It's Right" buttons for a vote pending. Beal arranged for me to participate in the World University Games. Carol Peterson, the best female athlete as UW majorette, is not in this picture.

I went to Brian's house to pick him up. By now, he was under 100 pounds, had lost all his muscle, and was firm that God chose him to be this way, to be an example of faith. I reached under him and picked up his limp body in my arms.

He looked up at me and said, "I am very happy to do this open housing thing; this is not right for the Blacks."

He was in pain just moving him, but he did not complain. I had known Carol from our dollar parties at the Sigma Nu house as a freshman. She was pinned by Gary Clark, captain of the football team.

At these parties, I was the best dancer in the house. So, when I arrived, everyone cheered. I went right to the stage, and the Wailers Band stopped. I yelled, "The party can now begin!"

Then, I leaped off the stage, did a split in the air, touched my toes, and exploded in dance. They rocked to their popular songs. Carol Peterson was doing flips, so everyone put us together, and boy, did we rock. I jumped over her head, and she threw her leg up and went backward into a split; everyone circled around us, hooting and screaming as the Wailers wailed.

She then disappeared with her pinned date. High energy! I love dancing and was the best in high school. Later on, I stopped going to these beer keg fraternity dollar parties. We would rent a huge hall where our noise did not disturb anyone.

From September 1st till my first meet at the Cow Palace on December 27th, I trained every day. Even on Sundays, when brothers in the house were recovering from their partying, I rose at dawn, ran through the ravine to Green Lake around Green Lake, back to the stadium, ran all the stairs, did 10 wind sprints, and then ran uphill to the fraternity. All out! No one was up yet, as it was just 7 AM.

Chapter 9: Beating Boston Once Again and Pulling a Hamstring

My time had finally come that 1963 fall. I was at the Cow Palace, and Ralph Boston was in the lineup, something I wanted, well over 130 days ever since I started my push to become the best-conditioned athlete in the world in my sport.

Deciding to make the Olympic team and go for the gold medal and not another world record, which still stuck in my mind. I had a familiar runway, plywood boards, fast and springy, but I knew to be cautious, get my steps right, hit the board, and get a fair jump. I had not practiced sprinting, except in the week before running in a large basketball gym in Spokane.

I had been invited to a "Man of the Year" banquet in Spokane—Rafer Johnson, Gene Fullmer, YA title and local heroes were present. I was honored for the first time and felt pleased to be an equal to these great athletes. I sat at the head table with my own nameplate. Everyone got some sort of award! It was cold, and there were several feet of snow in Spokane, which was unusual.

1963. Denny Spellacy introduced YA Tittle, Rafer Johnson, and Phil Shinnick at the Spokane Banquet.

Finally, my award came. It was a miniature wind gauge, a plastic hollow tube more like a thermometer. It said, "Wind or No Wind, You Are our World Record Holder." Everyone applauded, but it struck me the wrong way. I knew the wind was legal, but the popular story sullied it.

Apparently, the officials had voted to accept my record based upon all the evidence at the time—the hurdle race, its recording, all the official sensibilities, and my own and Brian's checking the wind. I smiled but was resentful. There was no use telling anyone about what had happened; it would seem like I was a sore loser, whining. Everyone does not like a sore loser, but I was not one. I was sore but not a loser. I eventually threw it away.

In the indoor 1963 Cow Palace meet, my turn came, so I cautiously ran down the runway and hit the board. However, I was a little off-timing, so I jammed my foot on the board, hurting my toenail. Yet still, I got a fair jump, awkward on the landing but 25 6' ½". This was a new Cow Palace record, and beat Ralph Boston for the second time, once outdoors and now indoors. I felt that I could go much further; I was not running at full speed. I did not know the indoor world record, but it started to enter my mind. Everyone sensed that I might try when my turn came. To be honest, I felt like my old self and had this feeling of letting myself go in my chest. They dimmed the lights, and the spotlight picked me out; I was ready.

Then I heard a voice from the darkness around the board track, "Phil, Phil." I ignored it; this happened many times and was a big distraction to me. This is always a problem when competing to stay within yourself and not be bothered by what is going on around you.

Finally, the voice persisted. I walked over to where it came from, and the spotlight shone on this athlete, who I will not name, who had been a member of a two-mile relay team at Modesto that broke the world record. The spotlight then shone on this athlete. I thought this was what he wanted, and I was not happy with this distraction. I thought to myself, *Pay attention.*

The pit looked short, and I felt that if I hit the board right, I would soar. This is what happened: I was fast on the runway and knew I would hit the board by my last jump, so I moved my steps back 6 inches to make sure. I had happiness in my heart even as I ran; this is what I sacrificed for.

About three steps before take-off, I surged to attack the board, everything just right. I hit a space between the underneath 2" x 4" studs on the edge supporting the plywood. It was like a trampoline; my right leg bounced up, even speeding up my runup. My hamstring contracted into a muscle spasm, a knot, but I was going all out and could not stop my leg from going forward. So, I ripped my hamstring and tried to straighten my leg, ending up on the far side of the pit, on the curved elevated boards on the turn. A foot race was going on, and I saw them just feet away, bearing down on me; an official pulled me off the track.

A day later, Phil Clark, S. J., high school math and coach for all sports, invited me to Alma to meditate in silence (he always had Christmas and Thanksgiving with my family). It was cloistered, so he took me to the radio shack where they had a communication ham radio. I slept on the wooden floor in a sleeping bag.

Alma is a retreat center for Jesuits south of the Bay Area. It is for those who have completed all their 12 years of priest training to meditate in silence. The pain was nearly unbearable; I turned over every 10 minutes until I found some relief. This would buy some time against the pain. I didn't mind the wooden floor, better than the cement I slept on in a vacant building hitching through Europe. I inspected my wound, and it was black and blue from ankle to buttock and swollen. I had ripped my muscle but also had torn blood vessels, which bled.

Here I was, all fall, figuring out how to deal with pain, and now it overwhelmed me. I suffered in silence and waited for dawn. I was starting my junior year, and the Los Angeles Olympic trials were now 9 months away. I had to get through a long qualification through the NCAA, semi-Olympic trials in New York in July, and September finals in LA, plus I had a complete dual season in the spring at Washington and a league championship. I could not walk without pain.

Most of all, I felt humiliated that I pulled my muscle under the spotlight and had to admit I thought about the world indoor mark. I decided I was not going to try to do that. Instead, just get through meets until the trails and get there healthy. This was a nightmare, and this marked a time when nights were spent just to get through and sleep dangerously. If I let myself go and went into a deep sleep, I felt that I would get off track and forget what was before me.

Nights were a time for prayer and to keep vigilance, and I knew I needed rest. But I did not want to! It was well known to everyone in the fraternity that if you walked by my bunk, I would be awake. I had put the bunk next to an open window and let the snow fall on my grandmother's quilt, which she made out of my grandfather's old wool suits, with sheep hair inside from their sheep on the farm.

It was comforting to breathe whatever weather and air was happening. I also watched the sky. If someone would stop or hesitate for a moment, I knew they were there, open my eyes, and have a conversation. This habit helped me later when I had two young girls who were up most of the night.

Later today, I see night as just the Earth's rotation and get up at about 2 AM. Then, I meditate for several hours, rest an hour or so, and get up early at 6:30 AM. In my early days, at dawn, I would take a long run and watch the sun come up. So, my Lunar meditation at Lao Fu was just my thing, meditating all night under the full moon.

That spring, in my college meets, I jumped just enough to beat the competitors, usually at 23' or 24', running slow and in control so as not to pull my muscle again. I would just take one jump and also wanted to set the Washington record for most points even though I was hurt. I knew that people were wondering what had happened to Shinnick; high school kids could now jump further than him.

My healing meant I would try to walk without a limp. As the blood receded in my torn muscle, I slowly jogged, day after day, slowly. Then, I did a gentle sprint with lots of stretching, week after week. In March, my season started, and I was not well yet. Three months and I felt the effect! My back hurt most of the time, and my foot had hairline fractures from hitting the board wrong with the slow approach. In the final Olympic trials, I wrapped two rolls of white tape on my take-off foot; after the event, I took my shoe off, and the tape was ripped, but my foot did not break.

Chapter 10: Recovering from a Painful Injury and Making the Olympic Team

My preparation for pain during the fall seemed prescient of my ordeal during the whole spring; each step hurt, but I knew I would never heal without circulation to my legs. At first, just walking to campus and down to the pavilion meant not showing pain, to walk as if not hurt. I feared that limping would upset my balance and throw my whole body off. It did, anyway. I spent time in the whirlpool, getting into the hot water, and every time, inch by inch at 105 degrees, I slunk slowly down.

At Comstock Pool in Spokane as a youth, getting into cold water was similar, but I still do not like to get into cold water or hot water. Later, when I joined a swim team at 50, it never got better; accomplished swimmers who do long workouts like to swim in colder water because they heat up. I had to sit on the side of the Columbia pool with my ankles in, dreading emerging. Then, as in Comstock, I had to count to 10 and hell or high water jump in— never to violate this oath. I learned this when I was young and awkward toward girls I liked; in the beginning, I would count to 10 and force myself to ask for a date.

Percy, the trainer, worked my hamstring like he did the year before when they froze after my three-hour knees-on-chest torture in the back of that station wagon. That took four months and never healed till I stretched my hamstring for nearly an hour before it let go. Here, it was bound and locked in reaction to the injury, and it did not want any movement. So, step by step, then faster walking, then slow jogging for hours.

The spring season was long, cold, and rainy, which was humiliating for me. I competed, never missed a meet (in my whole college career), and had long warm-ups and just one jump.

Since my run was slow, the timing was off, and I hit the board awkwardly and muscled my way through the take-off into the pit. I got to 25' this way. It mangled my toes and metatarsals by jamming. Faster runs mean quicker take-off. Finally, the NCAA Nationals came to Eugene. It was cold and windy there; I had to get into the top 6 in order to get to the July 1964 Olympic semifinal trials in New York. My warm-up was long, and my hamstring released some of it. But the danger was near at hand. If I ran too fast or pushed my jump, I might injure myself and then not recover in time for the July trials.

Finally, my time to post a good mark in the nationals came. I stood at the end of the run, ready to go, get a good mark or no Olympics. At that moment, it started to rain, and I was ready to go anyway; I had gotten my first 25' against the wind in the rain in Eugene, but here I was still wounded and could not use my strength or reinjure. I started my count to 10.

Bowerman stopped the long jump at that moment due to rain. He must have been watching as he said, "Go up into the stands."

I did what he said and sat with my brother, Nelson. We stayed warm and waited.

After about 45 minutes, while I slowly stretched my hurt hamstring and had two sweatsuits on to stay warm, they announced the long jump was now to begin, and the rain had stopped. After several wind sprints, not going too hard but waking up, my legs again stood on the end of the runway. This time, I did not hesitate. I ran the fastest I had run in 7 months ago and had a smooth, not-so-jerky take-off and not-too-bad landing, 25' 7".

After this preliminary round, I was second in the nation. The next day in the finals, I nearly matched my first day's jump, but it was difficult to jump two days in a row. I finished third. Sidney Nicholas went 26', and Gayle Hopkins jumped one of the best jumps ever behind Boston and me in the world at 26' 9 1/2". I made the semi-Olympic trials and had several weeks to heal.

I arrived in New York on July 4th, 1964, for the semi-Olympic trials qualifying round. It was hot and humid, over 95 degrees. I ran through my steps and sat down. I learned from St. Louis: why warm up when warm, just sit. My long years in the rain and cold meant every meet; I needed a long warm-up in St Louis that did me in. I was becoming a veteran, like Boston. My first jump put me right behind Boston in second, at 26' 1 ½". The top six went to LA for the final Olympic trials in September, which would give me two months to heal without jumping.

In other countries, I would not have been obliged to go through a season hurt and still get on the Olympic team. With my marks, any other country would have advanced me to the games. I just relaxed and did not have to jump again. My efforts were coordinated but not as far as my first jump. I was happy with the last few jumps. The 13 in the field was reduced to 6 for the finals. I was not sure about taking my last jumps; I would wait. The air had been still with a slight breeze. A zephyr came and blew hard; jumpers behind me now jumped further, one near 27', all a foot further than their best jump, wind-aided.

Boston increased his lead. In competition, wind-aided jumps count for placement. I moved down to sixth place, the last place. However, I was still safe, but I did not know that. I went all out because I did not realize I had already made the finals in LA. I was warm because of the humid soup I was in. I moved my steps back because of the wind and took off, feeling like old times, effortless.

My run was similar to my Modesto world record jump. It was effortless, like riding a horse, and I landed far out at the end of the pit. A great jumper, old Hawkeye Boston, was at the end of the pit; he largely ignored me during the competition. Yet, he watched every jump I took, waiting by the side of the sand pit to see my landing.

"About 27' 8"," he said.

Well satisfied, I looked up and saw a red flag. I checked my cleat marks, and I was over the take-off wood board by ½". There was a smudge in the putty put after the board to record going over. I maintained my sixth position and made the final Olympic trials. This encouraged me! It was very tense until I learned this. The heat warmed me up, so no warm-up was required. I just preserved my energy.

To get a decent mark, the runup needed to be in form and reserved. Then, I needed a fair jump and a decent mark. World record attempts are different; the form is gone, and so are all thoughts. The image in my mind was jumping out of a plane, pulling the ripcord, and letting go.

Letting it go means my strides are longer by inches, but these fractions of inches mean overextending the board. It is impossible to duplicate an all-out runup in practice; the only guesswork is how far to lengthen the approach. My leg held up. I would have a fresh start in the September LA finals Olympic trials.

I woke up not knowing where I was; I looked out the window of the bus, and the entrance to the LA Coliseum was all I could see. The bus parked, and I was at the Final Olympic trials in LA for Tokyo. The adrenaline ran through my body. I panicked because I had fallen asleep on the way to the trials from the valley we were housed in.

I could not compete this way. I was out of control and would be exhausted by the time I jumped in an hour. A grassy field opposite the entrance got my interest. It was warm. I did not need my sweats, and I had a white top and shorts on with a Washington uniform in my bag. I slowly jogged, trying to calm down. I ran about 5 miles slowly and finally got a competitive presence and relaxed; I did a few wind sprints, and the finalists in the long jump were called.

The six of us were introduced, and we walked abreast down the wide stairs onto the field. I measured my steps but did not have time to put my uniform on. I had a white tank top and cotton shorts, which I had trained in. I easily ran down the runway, not getting tense, and did an easy jump, 24'.

Terrible, I felt sunk. I walked over to the stands, and Lew Hoyt was there. He said to me, "Phil, you are walking down the runway."

I got the hint! For the next jump, I ran faster, making sure no foul, and jumped over 26' and was consistent and ended with 26' 3 ½". However, I did not go for a world record or all-out but just fair jumps. I was so fearful of a foul that I jumped off the tartan all-weather surface runway 12 inches behind the board. Boston had a great jump near 28' with some wind.

Only 1 ½ inches separated Hopkins (second) at 26 4 ½", me at 26 3 ½", and behind me Charlie Mays at 26' 2 ¾". I was Tokyo-bound, and all my pain and suffering had paid off. I redeemed myself and showed that I was not a fluke! I learned from Albuquerque and St. Louis by doing well in the New York semi-Olympic trials: if it's hot, why warm up?

Chapter 11: Getting Married and Leading the World University Games Team

I made a trip back to Spokane to see my parents and also my high school girlfriend, Sandra Etter, who had moved from Boone Street near Gonzaga U to the north into a bigger house. I had planned on spending time with her since we had a nice high school connection, were king and queen of the prom, and dated throughout high school.

I was 14 when I dated Sandra Etter. She was taller and outweighed me, but she also broke up with her older, handsome, upper-class boyfriend for me. I was a late grower and could not contain my good luck.

At 18, in our senior year, with high heels on, I was still taller than her and never forgot her trust in me at an early age. We were king and queen of the Gonzaga senior prom. When I went back to see her, I felt like Ulysses. I was not dead, but I definitely had been on long trips.

But as it happened, Sandra was entangled with another suitor. I had been away too long, which created an opportunity for other admirers. She was on the phone with this suitor from California who she had visited. He had been a suitor going to school in Spokane since her last years in high school. But I was there, and we were together. He waited.

During this visit, she could not get off due to his insistence on maintaining a course plan. I didn't know what to say, and a marriage commitment seemed premature. I left for Seattle to complete my mission and was not happy with the encounter. She had been a girlfriend through high school, and I thought we still had a connection. It seemed to evaporate, or perhaps we reached an impasse. I wanted to get out of Spokane, and she stayed.

I had to attend officers training school at Hamilton Air Force Base in the Bay Area in a week and the Olympic trials just a week after that. I needed to complete this challenge to redeem myself from the mischief of a track and field sportswriter. I felt I was a public disgrace and a black cloud over my world record. I always thought it unfair, given the legal conditions.

I thought that the Olympics and attempting to win in Tokyo would ease my pain. I felt I had no choice; I could not get off this goal. This nagged me in the back of my head. Before, I was someone I had felt close to for many years, and I was conflicted. I think first love is never forgotten! I faced this reality by putting it out of my mind or under the pile of challenges I felt I had to meet.

Back in Seattle, each day, I went to the Husky stadium to train. Its dirt track was fast this summer, and it had a lush green infield. It was the same situation each day: quarterback and fraternity brother Tod Hullin threw passes to Dave Williams, a star hurdler, meaning I did not have to run the hurdles and could sprint.

Carol Peterson, a seafarer princess from Queen Anne and Husky Rose Bowl Majorette, was pinned to an upper-class fraternity brother of mine. The most famous woman athlete in Washington and everyone's sweetheart. She was a senior, and I was starting my junior year. I did my speed work on the track, which ended with 10-speed barefooted wind sprints on the soft grass. I timed it to avoid Carol's twirling and Hullin's passes.

Carol came over to me as I finished and said, "Why don't you ask me out?"

She was a year older.

"You are pinned."

"Not anymore," she said.

I had a formal Air Force dance that weekend, so I called and asked her to come with me. She said she did not want to go to a formal dance. That was that! I learned from my fraternity brothers that she had gone to a show that night on a date with someone else. She approached me again and said, "Why didn't you ask me out again?"

I said, "I did, and you went out with someone else to a show and started to walk away."

I was slightly disgusted with her and felt taken.

She said, "I did not want to get dressed up, but the show was okay."

This did not make me feel better, and I walked away again, but she said, Why don't you call me again?"

She confronted me and stopped me from walking away. I looked at her. She seemed earnest, so I accepted her explanation and said, "Okay."

This situation was more open than my Spokane encounter.

Carol Peterson, Head UW Majorette at the 1963 Rose Bowl

I picked her up at her parent's Magnolia Hill house. The house had a panoramic view in all directions. I had to borrow a car. I walked backward up her front inclined stairs; the view was magnificent. She asked me to meet her mother and father; her mother was a Seattle Symphony concert cellist and piano player.

Her father greeted me with a hand but was missing four fingers on his right hand and just a pinky finger, cut off in a cedar shingle sawmill in college. He had wanted to be a sportswriter but is now public relations director for Red Cedar Shingle and Hand Split Shake Bureau. Her mother liked me. She had a grand piano, which caught my attention. I played piano for many years, at my mother's insistence (45 minutes a day for years), who could play Deep Purple. I kept looking at it. We left and got in the car. She sat not close, and there was silence.

She turned to me and said, "My mother said we would make great kids."

We looked at each other affectionately. My idea of being a Jesuit priest was dimming because I had to go into the military and make the 1964 Olympic team.

I stopped the car, turned it around, just blocks away, and said, "Let's go back and see your parents."

We told her mother, Jane, that she had a good idea and that both of us wanted kids. It was having the kids that got both of us. I disliked dating and had not gone out much for the past two years. We had never dated and had little kissing; we spent our free time with both our parents. I did not have much time before going to officer training.

The situation with Sandra Etter seemed too difficult, and I did not have time to go back to Spokane. Her younger brother, Ginge, had roomed with me in our fraternity and became the Husky quarterback.

Both Carol and I were virgins, and when we got married, we received a hand-painted parchment from the Pope blessing our marriage. I think Tom Toomey and Fr. Ameroult arranged it.

Carol knew all the reporters, so she got this on the front page of the Sunday Seattle Times.

Later, in 1965, Primo Nebiolo, an Italian official, invited me to Rome to compete after meeting him in Budapest for the World University Game (Universidad), a socialist-inspired game that played an international anthem rather than a national flag for the winners. Only student-athletes could compete. The US was excluded, and 1965 was the first US participation. I prepared and organized the whole delegation. I was recruited for the job.

Later, I found out that the CIA was involved in finances. Nebiolo flew Carol and me to Rome after the games. The field did not have a long jump or high jump pit, so I ran the high hurdles against Olympians Blain Lindgren and Eddie Ortiz. I think Nebiolo just wanted my company since we hit it off in Budapest. I thought about beating these wizard hurdlers.

Blaine, my buddy in Tokyo, told me the secret of high hurdling is that you attack the hurdles. I had not competed in Budapest as the leader of the delegation left no room. At 22, I was the youngest leader of a national team ever.

Harriet Beal had gone on to become a national officer with the National Student Association and said that a progressive athlete should lead the delegation. He also claimed that my open housing position was unique for a world-class athlete. I got the job after interviews in San Francisco.

1965 Budapest. Carol, Phil Shinnick, and John Pennel, Silver Medalist in Pole Vault

My first practice starts out of the blocks. I exploded, thinking I could challenge this stellar duo. I hit the first hurdle hard and nearly broke it. When the gun went off, I became more reserved for the first hurdle. They were three yards ahead of me from the start, so this was a big mistake; I held that distance but was third.

Blane was a silver medalist by a hair in Tokyo. He misjudged the finish while ahead since they had ten white lines at the finish. He dove for the first, resulting in the second silver being off-balance at the end.

I was in the locker room with him afterward. He picked up a huge bench and threw it, swearing, "Fuck everyone. Why did they have all those lines at the finish?"

Nebiolo said he was going to take us to the best barbeque in Italy. Carol and I were up for some fun after diplomatic meetings, and both were managing the team in Budapest. He brought along an assistant and another woman. I didn't know whether she was an official, but she seemed to know Primo. Carol was pregnant and having morning sickness throughout our trip to Budapest. We arrived after driving out of Rome and turned onto a farm; the chickens fluttered up, squawked, and ran in all directions.

Other animals were in this courtyard, not happy to move aside for our car. There was a cave, Quonset like an adobe, and we entered onto a long wooden table. Snacks and wine came out, but no one was there except us. I could see a barbecue fire pit deeper into the cave and a cook.

Cooked meat came on a big platter. Carol took one look at it, turned white, ran for a water closet, and threw up. She threw up twice, once from the meat and the other from the smell of the WC. This went on like clockwork with more types of meats. Carol was smelling it and running to the WC again.

Meanwhile, Primo's two friends got close; she snuggled up to him across from Carol and me on the picnic-like table next to Primo. She kept putting her tongue in his ear, and then they started kissing. Things became very heated. They had no room and slid under the table and kicked about. The table was shaking, and she came out of the end of the table. He followed closely, and both jumped into Primo's car and took off. I followed outside.

They gunned the car, and it swerved and headed across the dirt road to another field. The car smashed the gate, and the car stopped with the engine running; the doors flew open, and legs shot out through the open doors. The car rocked. I went back inside! Nebiolo said they would be out for a while.

This gave us time to talk without the two lovers and with no distractions except Carol running off to the WC.

Primo then asked, "So, what happened in Budapest? I heard you were arrested at the train station, and you drove your car up the stadium stairs and into the large hall where the certification officials were at a semi-circular table. You had one second to go before the deadline and had all the athlete's credentials stamped at exactly five o'clock. Everyone was talking about it; many did not want your delegation to compete. Big anti-American sentiment from the socialist community at the university games."

I told the story in detail.

It took me most of the summer in Philadelphia to get the uniforms, transcripts, and pictures into individual documents to become eligible. I needed a visa to get into Hungary, which I did not know about until a week before we left. When I called the Hungarian legation in Washington, the diplomat told me to send my passport in. They would send it back with a visa in two days.

By Friday, the end of the week, I had no visa and had no passport. I could not get a straight answer, and all weekend, I tried to reach someone, and when I did, they said they knew nothing about it. We got to Monday morning, the day of my flight, and still no visa or passport. I took the train to New York; our flight flew out in the late afternoon.

With all the athletes' uniforms, credentials, and our luggage, we arrived in a taxi in front of the passport agency in Manhattan. Carol waited in the taxi. It was a small office, and the line was next to the entrance door; my flight was one hour at JFK Airport, which was 45 minutes away. I saw a counter with a small hallway leading to a closed door. I pushed through the crowd, jumped over the counter, opened the door, and locked it behind me. A stunned official looked up.

In two sentences, I said I was a US Olympic athlete with all the certifications for the World University Games in Budapest, and the Hungarian legation had stolen my passports. I had no visas, and I had all the uniforms in a taxi outside and flew in one hour. Security guards banked on the door.

"Do you have a photo? Your name, address?"

"Yes, yes."

I had prepared. He pulled out a blank passport, typed in it, and then told the security guard to go away. I gave him my photos, and he stamped them. I pulled open the door. I then vaulted over the counter and ran out.

"Let him go," he says to me. "Make the flight."

Our lovers were still out in the field, so we had time to talk. Poor Carol was still sick from morning sickness, and the food kept coming. I felt very hungry and relieved to have accomplished my mission. However, I did not compete as I was too busy.

We arrived in Vienna to take a flight to Budapest, but with no visa, they would not let me board the aircraft. I heard of a train to Budapest along the Danube River leaving soon. We raced to the train station, got two tickets, and the train was set to leave in ten minutes. Each of my large suitcases weighed 80 pounds, and I had all the sports coat uniforms over my two shoulders. This was like old times on the farm with two 40-pound bales of hay in each hand. I was strong, but what train car did I get into to get the right train? Just then, an orange-uniformed Dutch official ran up to me and said, "You are Shinnick, I recognize you."

I told him I had all the uniforms and no visas. He said, "You cannot enter Budapest without a visa, but we can get you there. Come with me."

Carol could barely walk, so sick with morning sickness. She was white and on the verge of throwing up. The Dutch had their own two cars. The word got around among the athletes; they hatched a plan. Women and men about our size gave up their uniforms, and we took ours off and put on theirs; they then hid our luggage and clothes under other luggage. They had another plan: when they came around to check passports and visas in each small compartment, official passports that had already been checked were passed behind the back of the official. He just quickly looked at the passport and visas, so they figured he would not notice. It worked.

As we approached Budapest, we changed back into our US uniforms and got off the train; an official checked our passports and said you have no visas. He blew his whistle, and guards with rifles surrounded us. I told the Dutch friend to contact Jim Fowler and Nick Rodis, saying that I had arrived with all the certifications and uniforms. We were detained in some back room. Carol fell asleep on the luggage. She was entirely out of sorts and fatigued and sick. She laid over the top of our luggage in her formal dress, sound asleep.

Our lover friends came back very subdued, with hair a mess and clothes hardly on. They were still kissing, and I thought perhaps we would have another show outside. I went on with the story. I continued.

The deadline was 5 o'clock. At about 4:45 PM, we were let go, just enough time to miss the deadline. A huge Hungarian person loaded our luggage and said, "We will make it; it is a thirty-minute drive and rush hour traffic. I am Tibour; I will drive through hell to get you there."

He pounded his chest; he must have weighed three hundred pounds. "My father was killed on Margaret Island in 1956."

We tore out of the train station, and he was going over 80 MPH, honking his horn, when the traffic stopped. He went up on the sidewalk honking, and everyone jumped aside, not slowing down. In fact, he went against traffic the wrong way, never slowing down. I saw the stadium with its long stairs. He took the car straight up the stairs and pushed open the front doors with the car. I then raced inside the certification room with my briefcase full of documents for all athletes.

As I ran in, everyone looked at the clock; it read 30 seconds to 5 o'clock. I threw documents left and right to the ten people sitting around the semi-circular table. Stamp, stamp, stamp, each looking over their shoulder to the second hand. A second before 5, the last stamp occurred, and the US was at the World University Games, FISU.

Primo liked the story; the food kept coming, and Carol kept running to the WC. Just looking at the meat repulsed her. On the way back to Rome, I aired a gripe I had and told Primo, "I met the architect of the US entrance to FISU (student games) in a hotel room in Budapest."

He was a State Department official, James Fowler, and the student officer of the National Student Association was also there. Nick Rodis was smoking a big cigar in his boxer underwear. He told me we had to beat those communists.

He uttered, "Fucking communists, hit them over the head." Then, he flipped his ashes.

I attended the FISU congress as a delegate with Fowler, Bud Wilkenson, and Rodis. Toward the end, Fowler made a motion on the floor to certify both him and Rodis to be permanent US representatives to FISU.

"What was I, chopped liver?" I asked Primo.

"Wilklnson questioned the move and looked puzzlingly at me. We were left out. Both Fowler and Rodis were non-athletes, and anti-communists politically used Bud Wilkinson for their ploy. All my months of work was to get myself on the governing body."

I was not happy. There was no one to tell, but Nebiolo listened.

"I liked the international flavor of the games and all the athletes and officials I met," I told him.

In 1962, in Paris, I had the same good experiences with my socialist friends, going to Pamplona.

"Why the hatred?"

Later, after my first trip to China in 1976 to help China into the Olympics (why was China not in the Olympics?), I found that the third world had held the Games of the New Emerging Forces Organization in Indonesia, GANEFO, hosted by Sukarno (57 countries, 3000 athletes).

This was done to establish an anti-imperialist, anti-colonial sports force with unique cultural arts and crafts, including (like Apollo did with music, poetry, and medicine) in alternate years of the Olympic games.

The old order fought back and staged a military coup against Sukarno and murdered communists. This happened during the same time I was in Budapest. Rodis and Fowler were part of this reaction against socialist countries staging non-nationalistic culture—a prelude to the move into Vietnam.

Chapter 12: High Jumping to New Heights, Rain Storm at 64 Tokyo Olympics, No Good Jump

In 1965, my senior year, I was healthy, staying in shape, and not pushing for a world record. I did this so as not to get injured while amassing a competitive record for Washington that would go unmatched. This was what I wanted: to get in the record book by scoring more points than anyone in history.

Hiserman, my coach, put me in 5 events each weekend, anchoring the 4x100 relay, open 100, long jump, high jump, and triple jump. Our conference was the best in the nation; Oregon won the national title, battling with USC, and many Olympians I met in Tokyo competed in our conference. Carol's parents and my parents came to all my meets.

As the weeks went by, I became more and more beat up; I was jumping over 25' and 6' 8" in the high and long jump and posting fast 100 times against the top national sprinter in our conference. Many mornings before a meet, I complained to Carol that I did not feel up to competing in the meet. My back hurt, my sprint speed was dipping, and at the end of the season, jumping 25' was hard. I knew I could not extend myself too much or pull a muscle.

The NCAA nationals came to San Diego. I was spooked and, in Balboa Stadium, could not get over 24'. Or hit the board; in the open nationals, the long jump run was fast. Then, about 30' before the board, it turned to concrete with a new composition. My long spikes rattled, much like running with spikes on over concrete, and were slippery. I could not get on the board; it threw my steps off. I did not get a good mark!

The next day, I entered the high jump in the early evening. I was disgusted and in pain all over. So, I headed to the ocean and went body surfing. I spent three hours far out, catching waves and trying to forget my demise. I did not have goggles, fins, or a board; I just waited and shot through the bellow of these giant waves on my stomach with arms outstretched. I got sunburned, and it was thrilling.

The high jump had all the 1964 Olympic team and other 7' jumpers (about 30 in all 6' 10" and above), and John Thomas, my friend, former WR holder, and current American record near 7' 4", was there. The take-off was slippery under the hot sun, and the rubberized surface turned mushy. I made 6' 6", 6' 8", and 6' 10", and on my third attempt made 6' 11".

At 7' on my third attempt, I got over cleanly, looked down at the bar under my belly, and relaxed into the pit. For no reason, I reversed my trail toes, thinking it might get in the way, but it rotated up and hit the bar from underneath after my body got over. The bar rattled, and then, after seconds, it fell off. I had second highest height behind three jumpers, including Otis Burrell and Ed Caruthers, while beating John Thomas.

However, because I had more misses, I was 5th in the ranking, tying with Gene Johnson. It was won at 7'. This was an extraordinary effort, given I was tired, my legs flat, and I was sunburnt. Yet, these conditions made me stay in form and relax. My whole season was saved after my crummy performance in the nationals in the long jump. But now, high jumping is better than long jumping. This was Olympic team caliber in the high jump. I had never been so happy. Without that toe touch, I would have cleared 7' and made the national team in the high jump for international competition.

Instead, I went home and prepared for FISU or the 1965 World University Games in Budapest, and I was well satisfied. I was in the dog house with Olan Cassell, the US Director of US T&F (he had been on the opposite side of internal athlete's rights politics). So, I knew I would not be named to the national team, even though now I could compete in two events internationally.

We drove to Corvallis earlier in the season to compete against OSU. They had good athletes, and I exchanged first with their sprinter Rusty Brown in the open 100 and relay. In the long jump, I took just one jump in the mid 24's and won. The high jump was next. The take-off area was small, with hardly any apron surface, so we ran over slippery grass onto a very hard, cold surface. It was hailing, on and off, with rain, and the sawdust pit was rock-hard.

With arms and legs exposed, it scratched and cut. I started high at 6' 6", and one jumper cleared this with me, Dick Fosbury. I made the higher height with perfect form, approaching slowly so as not to slip. Fosbury went over the bar backward, ran from far away, and charged the bar.

As he went down backward after the bar on his head, I cringed that in the hard sawdust pit, he would break his neck. I had never seen anything quite like this under these conditions. Six feet-eight inches in the high jump was very good, and here was this kid jumping in the hail, easily over 6' 6", yet he missed a 6' 8". He wore baggy wool socks that had sagged and long hair. I stopped him and shook his hand.

I commended him by saying, "What a great feat making 6' 6" in these conditions." I really meant it because I was very impressed.

As porta pits came in and the apron of the take-off area far out, his approach became stable, and no danger of breaking his neck in the soft pit. He became Olympic champion at 7' 4" and revolutionized high jumping.

With my straddle form approaching too fast, it meant the knee would buckle under the stress: on higher heights, one's tendency is to speed up. The reason I did so well in Balboa Stadium is I approached the bar slowly, staying in form. This is extremely difficult because, looking at the bar, it seems impossible to jump that high—it is a mind game. I never looked at the bar on the approach; it was too scary.

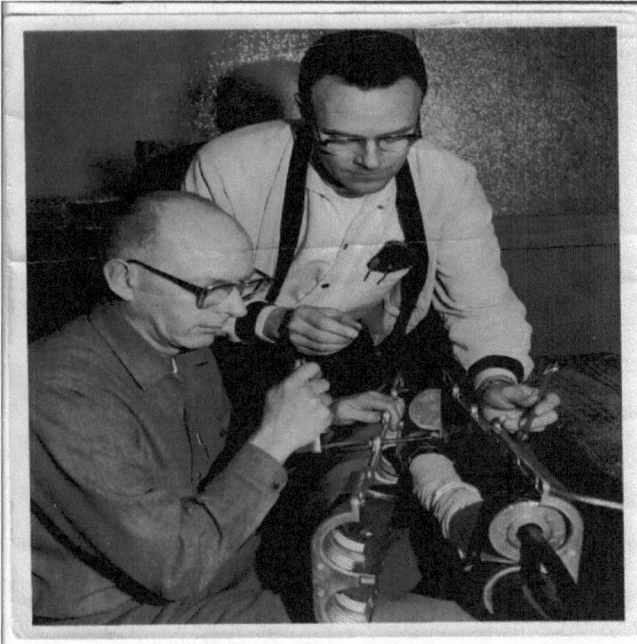

1959 Spokane, John Shinnick, and Ed McPherson, doing repairs.

By 1964, a Seattle executive moved my father to Seattle. Working at AT&T in Spokane as a cable splicer while holding the foreman's position for 12 long years, he still received no promotion. The Masons controlled all the senior positions, and he was a Catholic. Seattle AT&T executives, in their review trip to Spokane, asked why he was not promoted while clearly being the best.

They said, "Why promote him? He is our best foreman." He was also president of the AT&T Union.

After Tokyo, I was asked to attend a phone company gathering to honor my achievement in Seattle. The hall was packed, and my mother, father, and Seattle's top officers were on stage at the long table facing the crowd. I gave a speech saying it was the best experience of my life. I repeated this tale to all the news media. It was a great honor to meet all the top Seattle leaders, more so than even the Emperor of Japan. Everyone liked my speech; it was humble and showed how much I cared about my roots.

Seattle Pioneer Luncheon of AT&T Bob Davenport introducing Honored Guest John. Wilma, and Phil Shinnick 1964

In truth, it was the single worst experience of my life. Although once an Olympian, always an Olympian, this was a salve for my deep wounds from Tokyo. I never talk about it. No one wants to hear bad things, so I shut my mouth.

Instead, whenever someone asked how the Olympic team and Tokyo were, I would say, "The best experience of my life." This was my patent answer.

It was like hell for me, at best, purgatory. My self-criticism was over the roof. I should have never read *Dante's Inferno,* where Virgil escorted Dante through hell, purgatory, and paradise with the help of Beatrice. I began to feel this environment was like going through hell. My reading of Milton's *Paradise Lost* did not help. Since I had two roommates, Fred Hanson and his rice teammate, going to bed early.

I read Dante in a broom closet in the hall. Did this color my vision? Predisposed me? Olympians got $2 a day per diem; this was not automatic; you had to stand in line and only on certain days and hours.

On the proper day, I stood in line, and when it was my turn, the official said, "Sorry, come next week, the line is closed." I argued and was put off with disdain, summarily dismissed. It all started when Robert Giegengack, the men's head coach. He called all the Olympians together in a room in Tokyo.

With a Camel cigarette hanging from his lips and a hoarse smoker's voice in a Boston drawl, he said, "This is a dog-eat-dog world, and your teammates are competing against you for the Gold medal, and friendship is out here."

He went on and destroyed what good feeling I and everyone else had in the room of fellow US Olympians. I could feel the pallor come over the room, a quietness. He was saying, "Do not help your teammates; go do it alone. This Olympics is all about winning the gold."

Giegengack aborted the motto of the Olympics, "The important thing is life is not the triumph, but the fight; the essential thing is not to have won but to have fought well."

I believed in this motto; I was not enemies with fellow long jumpers Boston and Hopkins. And when I competed, I tried to get a good mark. I thought that I wanted to beat Boston or Hopkins at their best. What is a victory when your competitors are not right? Boston helped me with my steps sometimes, and we practiced jumping together in the LA valley. I liked Hopkins and had respect for his 26' 9 ½" at Eugene to win the NCAA. I could not jump that far then and was happy to get over 25' after my injury. I was hoping that all of us could get a medal. I rarely saw them again in practice after Gig's lecture and did not even know where they went to train.

Dore's Dante and Beatrice gazing from afar into Heaven's illumination. My vision of the Tokyo Olympics

I rarely saw them again in practice after Gig's lecture and did not even know where they went to train. I tried to train in the Olympic Village, but doing it while the visitors were in their glee was difficult. As I ran down the runway, these visitors walked across the runway, unaware of the intrusion one after the other. It was impossible in the village, so I went with my pole vault roommates to their training site. Other athletes were there, and the runway was fast.

All the coaches were on the field watching the pole vaulters; I asked one of the assistant coaches to watch my foot on the board as I ran through my steps. He did it once and said he needed to do a video of Hansen vaulting.

Four or five coaches were at the pole vault; it was a new event with the fiberglass pole, and these were college coaches like small kids around an ice cream stand. I was disgusted. It was impossible to find out where US athletes were training. I asked the English team where they were practicing, and they let me go on their bus, which was far away, to a terrible track with a bad runway and pit. They left me alone, so they were of no help to me.

It was time for our uniforms, and we had been measured top to bottom for special fits in Los Angeles. The day finally came; everyone was there. They gave me my uniform, which was a small size, both top and bottom. I heard fellow Spokane athlete Gerry Lindgren shout out, and they gave me a large one. I swapped with him; it was medium and too short.

Everyone was shouting that I got the wrong size; everyone was going up and down the hallway, trying to find a fit. The officials had just guessed what size we were. I am 6' 4" and 180, so I knew the officials did not know who I was. These officials, to me, felt like they were Gestapo, bossing us around like small children. Why did they measure us? It seemed that the uniform company just sent lots of sizes but never took the pains to follow the measurements we sent them.

Completely disheartened, I went to an official, and they said, "Do not worry, these can be tailored."

My small bottom competitive warm-up uniform came back extended. When I put them on, I walked, and the bottom around the calf was too small, so I rotated around. This made it very uncomfortable.

On the day of my competition, October 18th, 1964, I could not sleep much because Hansen had just won the gold medal and left the light on. He had spent hours by the mirror basking in his gold medal and Olympic record, so I could not move him out of his trance.

Finally and hurriedly, he went away. I woke up and hurried to breakfast, thinking that a good meal was necessary for the long day of preliminaries. I went to the bus area, and it left without me. I knew that no coach or officials had helped me or even cared about my presence.

I thought I'd just take a cab to the stadium, which I did, and the cabbie took some time to find the competitor's entrance. I arrived and saw Boston and Hopkins start to go to their pit for prelims. I was late. I started to go with them and was told I was at another pit on the other side of the field.

When I got there, the clearance for the warm-up area indoors was about 6' 2". The Japanese are small, so I could not warm inside. I went outside, and it was cold and raining. I had my tape measure to measure the exact steps I had worked on so as not to foul. I just need a jump to get me in the top 12 for the finals. The Japanese officials would not hold the steel tape for me. I looked around and could not get the attention of the other athletes. I could tell that it was I that they eyed; they had to get by me and ignored me.

I went to the track and put one foot in front of the other, assuming that one of my feet was afoot. I counted out 135 steps, then eyed the runway and put a metal marker by the side of the runway. I could just run through my steps like all the other jumpers were doing. Halfway down the runway, an official stood in my way, so I thought I'd run him down, and he would move so I could get my steps; he didn't move, so I swerved to the side. I had no steps.

I would be running blind. Steps are the single most important thing in the long jump; the board is just 8", and the runup is 135'. Now, it was raining so hard that I could not see; the water was dripping into my eyes. I would be running with no steps, and I could not see. I still thought, *I will do it.*

As I started, the wind blew hard at my back, so I had to be careful not to foul. I thought of a new Olympic record, which was 26' 5" by Jesse Owens. I could do that on my first attempt. I had a great jump. The red flag went up, and I was fouled by a hair. Still, I had two jumps to make the finals; the runway was muddy and soft, and the area around the runway was underwater.

In my second jump, I felt the wind shift; it was directly in my face. So, I moved my steps up a little, ran well, and took off with a fair jump. I needed one to make it past the prelims, but I jumped off the muddy runway way behind the board by at least a foot. Still, there was one jump left!

At the end of the runway, the wind shifted to my back. So, I tried to make an adjustment. However, when I went to look at the marker where I had started from my last jump, it was gone! Someone had taken it, and I had no steps at all. It became apparent to me that all the forces of nature and men were against me as I stood at the end of the runway.

I decided that what I needed to do was jump far and show the world what a great jumper I was; I was going to go all out and try to break the Olympic record. The wind was constant at my back. I got a great jump toward the end of the pit and felt the board under my foot.

Again, a foul! Would I make the finals with that jump off the muddy runway far back? No, I was out of the competition. Later, officials brought me the wind gauge readings. As it turned out, I was the only competitor from all the countries that had completely opposite wind to front and back at nearly 12 miles per hour, a very stiff wind.

The rain did not let up. From the other pit, Boston, Hopkins, and Wariboko Queen Boy West from Nigeria, my teammate at Washington, made the finals. Most did from the other pit! I found out that since Hopkins beat me by ¾" in the US trials, he and Boston could go to the good pit, and I had to go to the pit for those low down in national ranking.

Yet still, my jump in the trails was in the top 10 in the world at that time. Wariboko West jumped 25' 5" in 1963 before my Modesto meet, getting second to my 25' 6" and jumped 23' at Modesto behind my 27' 4". He ended up fourth in the Olympics in Tokyo at 24' 11". He was the first jumper for Nigeria, so he got to jump with Boston and Hopkins.

My idea for my last jump was just to show the world good form and a great jump. It did not count, but that picture was taken around the world. It wasn't put in the caption that I did not make the finals. But I treasure it because it is just a very good picture.

1964 Tokyo Olympics. Associated Press Release World Record breakers Brummel, Szmidt, and Shinnick: The Russian Valery Brummel lands after his high jump of two meters. Poland's Josef Szmidt is also in good form (left). Broadjumper Phil Shinnick, USA, seems to want to fly like Icarus.

In the picture, my hips raised level with the railing in the first row of the stands some 10' up, and in the background in the stands, all you could see were umbrellas and rain. This picture showed my shoelaces black from the mud when my foot sank in the mud. The picture is what I imagined when all the forces were against me. Then, at least, I can show the world my ability and good form. This photo was kind to me.

Brummel and his wife, Elana Petuchokov, became intertwined in my life. He had a model high jump form, which I adopted. Elana and John Thomas were cohorts in Soviet and US friendship exchanges to mute nuclear proliferation in later years. He suffered a compound fracture in a motorcycle accident of his take-off leg, and I visited him in Moscow after the accident.

.

Chapter 13: What Color Is Shinnick? Dante And Beatrice in The Inferno Seemed My Experience at the Olympics

The US Olympic delegation order rank went by height and by alphabet in marching into the 1964 Tokyo Olympics opening ceremony. The United States of America meant we marched into the stadium near last, and the USSR was in the same boat. The outside parade ground was massive, holding all the delegations waiting to go in. It was clear and slightly cold.

By height, I lined up with the basketball players, weight men, and high jumpers. I stood next to Bill Bradley, Al Oerter (at this time, two-time gold medalist), and John Thomas. My ill-fated injury in the Cow Palace, not quite a year ago, as well as having to compete all previous spring, left me with a backache most of the time.

Standing for any length of time was murder for me! I wore a corset-like back brace under my parade uniform of white hat and blue blazer, with a gold embroidered emblem on the pocket in Japanese with the Olympic emblem, US insignia, and white pants. The back brace had 8 steel inserts that ran the length of the corset. It kept my back warm and helped with the pain of standing. Running, walking, sitting, and lying were okay, but standing was difficult.

We were on the parade ground longer than most other delegations because we were near last. I was not comfortable. I stood on one foot and then another. Across the field, we could see the Soviets. We nervously checked them out, and a whisper went around that the Soviets were directly across the field from us; they had light brown dress uniforms, and their delegation was as big as ours.

Opening ceremony Tokyo Olympics 1964 US delegation

US officials lined up in the front ranks; they seemed to be studying the Soviets and moving about in the front ranks before we went into the stadium. They broke ranks and circled around to the side as if in a huddle; an official of the Soviet delegation was walking toward the US team. What were the US officials to do? They decided that the sole Soviet official stood still halfway between the two teams and motioned for someone to go forward.

Reluctantly, a US official walked out to see what they wanted; there was a brief interchange, then officials circled while powwowing back at our delegation, and they spread out, going through the ranks of the athletes.

Everyone wondered what was up! Officials walking between ranks were questioning the athletes. I asked Thomas if he could hear what they wanted. He turned to me and said, "Phil, they are looking for you."

An official walking between our lines buttonholed me, saying, "They want you, the Soviets want to see you."

I broke ranks to the side; the leadership circled around me and said, "They want you to walk out away from the team, at least 20 feet, take off your hat, and wave to the Soviets."

They wanted to see who broke Ter Ovanejan's long jump world record. When I got back in the ranks, Oerter, Bradley, and Thomas wanted to know what had happened, so I told them. Thomas said I think they want to see if you are Black; they maintain that the US could not beat the Soviet team without Black athletes. Taking off my hat was necessary to see my color.

Five years later, in Moscow, after I recovered from my injury, they recorded and measured a leap of 28' 6" indoors. Just before my great leap, intense lights and cameras rolled, and I was blinded 15' from the board as the lights turned on, so I jumped blinded and was not able to see the take-off board; I could not see the board.

I landed about a foot and one half past a red flag to the side of the pit and thought, *Well, I broke the indoor stadium record. Pretty soft!*

It was the World Indoor Record. They announced the length of the jump. A foul did not matter; they were happy to see such a great leap. The long jump winner should be the athlete who jumps the farthest from take-off to landing. But they had this rule, not over the front line of the wooden board. This was easy to do; we did it in grade school.

Later, in this 1969 Moscow Indoor Competition, I slowed my approach down to make the finals. Ter Ovanejan and their other great jumpers were in the field. They called me "The Great White Horse," and when I returned on peace missions 20 years later, my leap and name stuck. Ordinary people remembered that night and the distance and still called me the Great White Horse. I have always received the red-carpet treatment in Russia!

Later, Giegengach was no longer seen after his attack on the spirit of the Olympics and my sense of fair play; he spent his time with Wendel Motley, a Trinidad 400-meter runner and a member of his Yale team. The other coaches were from colleges and had never coached world-class athletes, spending their time videoing the pole vault for their college kids. I saw the effects of this speech: team members avoiding each other and a breakdown of spirit. His mantra was seeking the gold, so those who failed were ignored; after Fred Hansen won his gold medal in the pole vault, he wanted me to accompany him to interviews.

We went to a Japanese radio station for his interview. My presence was noticed, and they asked who I was. Next, a Japanese man came over to me and said you go sit over there away from the cameras. You did not win the gold. They put me in a dark corner of the studio. I felt the Olympics and media had lost their ideological way, and the games were nothing more than nationalism and an obsession with gold.

Dante's journey through hell for me was the Olympics, and I did not even get to purgatory; no Beatrice to help me get past hell or purgatory. I could see the effect of this perversion on those who, for reasons of injuries, weather, or just getting boxed in during a race, did not get medals. Also, they were dogs with tails between their legs, ignored, reminded of their failure by ignoring them to win any medal.

The 1964 Olympic team, the week after the games, traveled to Osaka for a meet with Asian, Australian, New Zealand, and South and North American select athletes. It was a big meet with a packed stadium. I did not attend the closing Tokyo Olympic ceremony; athletes who did not win told me later it was the best part of the games and washed away bad memories. I felt I did not deserve to be in the closing ceremony, so I stayed in my room.

In Osaka, only two could compete in each event, and since Boston and Hopkins had gotten into the finals, I was out of the long jump. One of the coaches came to me and said I could run the high hurdles with Blaine Lindgren, my closest friend from the Olympics. I felt this was a reprieve for me, so I started my physical and mental warm-up for the hurdles, which I had not run for over two years.

To me, no practice, in any event, meant nothing; if I could keep form, that is all that mattered, and I could do that. In high school, for the first time ever running the event in practice, I beat the city record in a time trial.

No problem for me and a new opportunity; the same official came back later onto the field and said, "You cannot run the high hurdles since Rex Cawley (Olympic champion in 400 hurdles) wants to run the high hurdles, Bob Hayes is not here (Olympic Champion in the 100 meters), and we want you to run the first leg of the men's 4x 400-meter relay. Ashworth will run second, Stebbins third, and Henry Carr last."

Out of hell and purgatory for me with a reprieve. I had the same feeling before Modesto after my aborted great jump that morning in Berkeley. There was justice in the world; I felt it, and all my bad feelings about Giegengach and the violation of the Olympic spirit washed away. I was given the baton by an official and assigned to the first lane.

From there, I would be able to see Jamaica in lane two, our main competitor. It was a dirt track but fast. Ashworth and I paced off the exchange zone, and I told him that I would be coming like a bat out of hell. I meant that! He rolled his eyes toward me and thought from his face I was a weak link; I could sense his disappointment that Hayes could not run.

I got a perfect start and could see the Jamaican five yards ahead with the stagger; the whole race was in lanes. I hugged the inside curb and had the same feeling as in Modesto: happy and all out, free, with no thinking. I made up the stagger, it seemed, in ten strides and flew by him to take the lead. I felt as if I was pushing from behind, not even feeling my feet on the ground; it was just one long surge, like that Great White Horse cutting off the bull for his escape to the woods. All out!

I saw ahead that Ashworth was not taking off and waiting. I thought he was thinking, *Here comes this slow guy, make sure of a good pass. If I slowed down, I might go up his back.*

Should I jump over him and hand him the baton, I thought.

And he had not put his hand out yet. I just ran by him so as not to crash, turned, looked him in the eyes, he had a startled look, gave him the baton in front of him, and yelled, "Go, go go!!!"

It was a legal handoff within the exchange zone. Ashworth ran hard, as did Stebbins and Carr; the time was near the world record, but I felt my exchange with Ashworth lost several tenths of a second, and I wanted a world record.

The Olympic coach who put me on the team nestled up to me, showing his stopwatch, stated, "Phil, you ran 10.1 just off the world record in the 100 meters, and you ran around a turn. This is the fastest ever recorded on the first leg. Other legs had running starts; you ran out of the blocks."

I was out of hell, passing quickly through purgatory to Heaven in 10.1 seconds, and my whole trip to Tokyo became better. I had bad dreams about that day of my Tokyo jumps; all the forces of nature, officials, and competitors thwarted me for 40 years. But this day, I was redeemed! I felt it deep inside me. This relay was not remembered back in the US, but I knew that my teammates saw what I could do and that there was respect missing from the games that the fans in Osaka saw.

Before the games, training in the Los Angeles Valley, Boston, Hayes, myself, and a few other Olympians played football on the lawn. Old Hawkeye (Boston) was passing to Hayes; I was guarding Hayes. I stayed with him and batted down Boston's passes so Hawkeye became more accurate. Hayes got tricky, and Boston threw the ball away from me. Down, Hayes dove for the ball. I could not believe how good his hands were. Most sprinters have wooden hands. Hayes was spectacular, and I also saw what a great athlete he was, but I could stay with him. Unless, of course, a pass was away from me and down. It was a great privilege to replace him in Osaka.

I wanted a rerun of the Olympics and started thinking of Mexico City when I was eliminated. However, I had my senior year ahead of me, which, in the end, destroyed my chances for an off-Olympic year national team due to fatigue and pain.

As a reward, 30 years later, I was inducted into the UW Hall of Fame. Brian made it within five years; I was excluded due to my politics. Later, I was called an ideological dissident. It started with my negation of Giegengach's dog-eat-dog philosophy, which I found repugnant. The word out was that he was an intellectual and knew Latin; I had two years of Latin plus years of a Latin mass and wondered what was so great about that when he talked, his lower belly stuck out further under his shirt.

Sport to him was intellectual, and all the officials thought he knew something about truth; they followed him like an alpha wolf. I saw him as a person who did not understand what is in an athlete's heart and the essence of the sport since he ignored his own body.

Chapter 14: Finding Another Life in Intellectual Work, John Lui, A High Jumper I Coached Was Killed

In my own nature, I wondered if all the obstacles I faced in the long jump and world record leaps that did not officially count due to going over the board were my resentment, somewhere hidden in me or in the forces in nature against me. If I received an official world record in the long jump, subsequently, it would mean that what happened in Modesto would be moot and injustice forgotten. Did, somehow, I prevent this with the help of tempest nature this honor since I feared honor would put me before the last judgment, not worthy of heavenly presence, grasping for honor and forgetting goodness?

Self-aggrandizement and concupiscence became our tendencies to self-destruct over fame and honor. Yet, in my heart, I am an athlete, and this is what I do and care about. Other running or field events might be better for me.

This changed, and my obsession with this dishonor changed. I sat in an advanced economic history class. Up to my senior year, all classes had hundreds of students, and breakout sessions were 35 to 40. I never talked with a professor that I thought that was cheating. I suffered in an advanced microeconomics class. The teacher gave us a thick graduate text on econometrics. He told us to read it.

All quarter, I went down onto campus on weekends and read the whole text for over 10 weeks. I outlined it. Difficult and technical. I did above average on the lead-up test. I must have flunked the final since I got a D in the course. Some fraternity crew athletes came to me and learned I got a D. They all got As and told me they went to the professor early as a group, and he said that the textbook for the final or even previous exams was not on the test, forget the text. He told them what was on the exam; they did not study. The key question was, "How do you determine whether to buy raspberries or strawberries?"

I built an aggregate indifference curve with arbitrary prices to start with and showed how supply and demand prices would shift the taste consumption of the two berries. I learned this from this text. Very complicated but on the mark. These crew athletes said the answer was one word, "Taste!" How could this be? Shortage from bad weather of either crop changed supply and price, and this would affect taste.

Several years later, I went to the head of the department, Philip Cartwright, who told me, "You had the right answer. Why didn't you come to me? I heard about your work."

In this advanced class, I sat in the back of the small room of 8 students, and Robert Thomas, the economic history professor, walked in, took one look at me with my athletic award sweater on, eyeing me for some time.

"You wear your award as an athlete on your sleeve; this is an economics class," Meaning he did not like athletics and was short, slightly portly, and an academic.

I promptly retorted, "Dr. Thomas, should I call you Mr. Thomas so you can renounce your own achievement, receiving a PhD?"

He looked at me for some time, then said, "I dropped a battery on my foot, I bought a gas station, it is all swollen, and I am limping and in pain."

He was saying he was in a bad mood because of his pain. He smiled at me. We became great friends, and my life was about to change. He told me he was doing work in the auto industry during the 30s and asked me why I didn't do a study to compare a farmer getting a new truck versus the old way of taking the harvest to market by horse and wagon.

With another student and my knowledge from reading that whole microeconomics test, we did the study, creating an equation, amortizing a truck, horse, and wagon over time, then pricing hay and gas and average distance to the market. We learned it was inefficient to have a truck due to the price of gas and maintenance, which did not allow for an hourly shorter time to market.

He came to me and said, "Forget this class! You will get all As in the next two classes."

I worked during spring break in the auto industry with a calculator. I will give the equation, and you can crunch the numbers. At that time, you had to crank the numbers with a lever on the side of the machine. He also gave me the manuscript from Alfred North, a senior economist professor, in long hand to take with me for the indoor nationals in Detroit.

At the indoor nationals, no one was near me, and with an average performance in the long jump, I could win. I spent the whole time in my room reading North's manuscript, the only copy. Thomas wanted my honest opinion. He told me I had the background. Page by page, I went over his equations and data, and, in the end, I had 20 pages of criticism in my own notes. I was very happy!

From those pages in my hotel room to the competition across the street, I arrived just in time for the long jump. I jumped 25', stayed in form, and did not deviate. Coles from Maryland beat me by a fraction of an inch. I did not care or even attempt to beat him. I found a new love. I entered graduate school in public affairs and delayed my commission in the Air Force for two years.

Hiserman extended my scholarship for another year, and I could coach the high jumpers. Carol was pregnant and due in the spring. I had 13 papers due in the fall, so this academic life was good. I had small classes and liked learning about foreign aid, national security, and administering large agencies through case studies.

Hiserman, a couple of years earlier, asked me to look at a new recruit from a small town in southern Washington, a Native American. I am not sure what tribe he came from, but he was high school state champion in the shot and discus. I watched him in an exhibition and then met him.

He was my height and only a little heavier, yet when he threw with an explosion by putting himself into another state of being. I liked his intensity, like a balloon popping, when he threw. Deep wavy hair and eyes that scoured looking right through you. He checked me over, said little, and spoke slowly and purposefully.

"Come to Washington, and you can be in my fraternity, and I will be your big brother."

He hesitated, walked in a circle, then said, "Okay, that is it. I pledge Sigma Nu." And then, he became my little brother and roomed with me.

After he won our PAC 8 conference in his sophomore year with a throw near 190', I thought he could make the Olympic team. He had a lot of anger.

One day, he was really mad and could not express it, but he was about to explode; I could see he was ready to fight. So, I pushed him in his chest. Everyone was afraid of him. "So, Al, what are you going to do?"

He backed off; he knew I was his match, was my little brother. He loved me. He then confessed his anger. I found that he was not getting the grades he deserved in the PE Department. I snooped around and found out that the professors saw him as a dumb Indian and gave him Cs regardless of his exam grade.

At this rate, he would not have become a Sigma Nu member without better grades. I urged him to take regular classes and get away from this racism. He did! He signed up for geology and economics and got good grades; he was smart.

During my coaching, I retrieved his discus and shot puts in practice, and he taught me how to throw. I gave up the long jump in graduate school. Al had no high school coach who learned the form himself; like me, Hiserman never coached me during my undergraduate eligibility days. I had been elected team captain as a sophomore, so he just complained to me about underperforming teammates each day as an undergraduate. The only information about my performance was a posted workout each practice day and what events I would run on the weekend. No advice on my high and long jumping or hurdles and sprints.

Hiserman extended my scholarship after I graduated to help coach the team. I had one good high jump potential. John Louie, a small Asian, about 5' 8", but a good high jumper, only once making 6' 6".

Day after day, no matter what I said, his left foot turned in on take-off at a higher height. If he could make 6' 8", he would be competitive; he was stuck in a bad habit. The higher bar spooked him. I showed him how to do a one-legged squat, and in two months, he could do it. He was ready; he had the strength now. I had time to practice the high jump that year.

On days, I would put the bar just above the world record at 7' 6" and attempt it. I could get over the bar, but on top of the bar, I would make some moves that toppled the crossbar. The form changes as you jump higher, and I have not quite figured it out. I had one competition in an all-comers meet, and I made 7' 1/2". John Louie was like this; he did something different at higher heights.

One day, that morning, I devised a new plan: make him jump without a bar and use proper form, keep his plant foot parallel to the bar, and not turn in. When he did not turn his foot in, he soared at low heights.

"John, now, I am going to put the bar up, and I do not want you to look at the bar. Just plant your take-off foot parallel to the bar and do not rush the jump; let it happen, and do not rush or try harder."

I put the bar to 6' 6". He went over with ease; I put the bar up to 6' 8" or 6' 9".

"Now, do the same thing: do not look at the bar. Keep your form only!"

He approached the bar in the same way and cleared it by several inches. He was now a national-class athlete. Finally... he landed in the pit, exclaiming, "John, you made 6' 9"."

His arms went up in the air, he was angelic, he glowed, his head was raised to Heaven in gratitude, and he jumped out of the porta pit toward the shot-put area indoors in Hec Edmundson Pavilion, on the dirt floor. We had a barrier up blocking off the shot put. He jumped over the barrier, arms overhead, in a trance of joy, as if winning the Olympic championship, an unbelievable feat. He stayed in this state in another world, chest out, arms up in gratitude. I whistled with my hardest whistle, which could wake the dead. I screamed, I yelled; he was gone into his own world. I ran toward him.

Al Pemberton released the shot put, and I saw he had a spectacular throw, arching high. Louie was gone into his head; it hit him square in the side of the head, the sound, terrible, now with me. I rushed to him, and his skull was smashed in on the side. He would not live; I knew this. His brother, Bob, was hurdling nearby and ran over. I put a towel over the wound, and his body was twitching. And now, I had to tell his parents, who owned two restaurants in Seattle, about the funeral. How could I explain Brian and now John Louie?

These tragedies and my own dishonor over my great leap stunned me and moved me away from sport. I did not think this was divine providence, karma, or fate. I still do not understand this, and it reminded me of my car accident, my cancer, and how fragile life is. I think John's family lost one of the restaurants, and I do not think the family has ever fully recovered.

Al never threw the shot again and never improved in his discus throwing; he got a job with a bank, married, and had a beautiful girl. His daughter said he still had anger (drinking changed his mood), but when he looked at her, it dropped, just like me. She knew he would never hurt her. I knew the same!

I tried to find him in the last ten years, and he died before I located his family, but he connected with his daughter. I told her story after story about him, and she was like a child hearing a bedtime story, completely transfixed, living inside my stories. She said it was the happiest time since she never knew about John Louie or fraternity life, and it gave her a deeper understanding of how he was and the ghosts he had to carry.

Chapter 15: Working for the Mayor of Seattle, Senator Jackson, and Vietnam War Hawk, Bobby Kennedy as Friends and Supporter, Going to the Decathlon

After my graduate assistant coaching year finished, Bob Flowers, former captain of the UW basketball team, and I were named municipal government interns and given offices just off the large Office of the Mayor of Seattle. It was occupied at the time by Dorm Braman on the top floor of the municipal building. Guests of the mayor would walk out of Braman's office and come down the hall off our office. Scoop Jackson, Washington US Senator, exited from the Office of Mayor of Seattle (1967). I buttonholed Jackson, and he didn't seem to mind; he knew who I was!

Pleasantries then got to my concerns, Vietnam; I went through the plethora of my thoughts, the domino effect, far off in Asia, the French's unsuccessful adventure. He let me continue; he'd heard this before. I said it all, and I paused.

"Listen, Phil, here is what we are up to! We have many weapons we have just developed, and now we need to see how they work, such as napalm armored helicopters and better missiles off aircraft carriers. This is the real story! We need to go after the communists."

Senator Jackson was on the Armed Services Committee and was a war hawk but liberal on all domestic issues. My brother Nelson had signed up to be a Marine officer. That year, before they escalated the war, he was in pilot school.

After graduating, he was assigned to the war zone and flew 800 combat missions in Vietnam as an armored Huey helicopter pilot, one of the deadliest aircraft devised. It had eight rockets, two 50-caliber machine guns, and napalm weapons. Jackson authorized this aircraft. Nelson's life was forever changed. He and three others out of 30 who deployed with him came back, and those other two took their lives.

This disheartened me to hear him talk. I had been to socialist FISU, the student university games, or the 1965 Universidad and met his socialist enemies who pushed internationalism and sport with art and music, dancing, and against nationalism, which separated people. This all seemed fine to me! Senator Jackson's holster held the triggers to these weapons.

Fifteen years later, I was returning from a peace mission to Moscow, about 5:30 AM at JFK, and read in the early morning newspaper that a reconnaissance plane with civilians on board was shot down over the Soviet Island off of Alaska. I was on my way out from New York after being in Moscow on a flight to Seattle.

Later in the day, the story changed; now, it was a regular civilian aircraft with congressmen and members of the right-wing John Birch Society on board. All were killed! I knew Scoop was part of this, but he was *not on board.* He was then in Seattle, so I decided to go talk to him the next day about this after I landed in Seattle.

The next morning, on the way to see him, I heard on the radio that Scoop Jackson had died early that day. I wanted to talk with him. *Did he get killed to avoid a scandal, or was the pressure too much for his brain?* I did not think folks read the early editions in the East about the surveillance equipment on board.

Just a month later, outside the hall of the mayor's office, the same scene. Senator Bobby Kennedy had just talked with the mayor, and it was just him and me in the rugged hallway exiting the mayor's office. Same speech but more rehearsed.

He smiled at me and said, "Congratulations on your jump and the Olympics. I agree with you; it is a misadventure, and no good will come from this. Can you come with me to a rally later in the day? I'd like you to sit next to me."

This was 1967, and he was running for the presidency, or thinking about it, we went to an auditorium, a raised stage with a dais and a bunch of metal chairs. I sat next to him, and he introduced me. Then, he gave a speech about stuff that was also on my mind but with more conviction: no Vietnam, the racial issues, poverty, and he went on and on about injustice. He would be my friend. I knew it, and there was a connection.

In Seattle, there is a long tradition of Republicans and Democrats working together for the good of the city. Mayor Braman, a Republican, had an open office and was very popular, so all the Democrats and Republicans flocked to him.

In the mornings, I went to work in the mayor's office, reviewing the capital improvement document and setting priorities while learning what projects the city needed to be done. I also worked in the civil service validating examinations.

In the afternoons, I had classes and would literally run over to the stadium to run a little, but I had no serious training and no plans to compete again. Walking home was difficult from the stadium; I was exhausted and had migraines, which lasted a day, then later two or three days with headaches. Not enough time to eat during the day.

Carol usually had a big meal for me when I got home, and Shannon was a little over a year old. Carol was teaching batons to high school baton twirlers and, in the summer, went to a camp in California to teach; both our parents were nearby. We moved to a larger apartment in an attic about a mile from campus, but when I opened the door to the apartment, it had not been lived in for what seemed years, all dusty and dank. It was only $75 a month, but I had to fix it up. A friend and I looked at it and decided it was too hard to clean, so we painted over all the floors and ceiling with 12 gallons of paint and then put down a linoleum floor. It took days to dry!

We moved in, and there was a big closet where we put Shannon to sleep; she was approaching a year now. Yet, Shannon and later Quincey, our second girl born in Los Angeles, walked or, better to say, ran around at seven months.

When the relatives found out that we put Shannon in a closet, this became a big joke. Carol had a hard time chasing Shannon, and then later Quincey running around. Both became champion athletes and All-Americans and went to college on athletic scholarships.

I got a call that there was a decathlon in Trail, British Columbia, above some mining sites. *Would I come?* Since I did not have to jump 26' and do all the events without practice, I could do it except the pole vault. Yes! I did a week of sprinting.

In the 100 meters at Trail, BC, I ran faster, a tenth faster, after conversion than Harry Jerome, the world record in six events in sprinting, and silver medalist at 100 meters, 10.7. He ran 100 yards at 9.9. I knew he was cruising; the track was slow, and I felt encouraged.

Nevertheless, the long jump sand pit was only 24', so Nelson, my brother (before he went to officer's training camp), took a shovel and spaded the pit to go 25'. He groomed the dirt some. I jumped right to the end of the pit at 25' into the dirt and stopped. Too dangerous!

In the decathlon, you only get 3 attempts instead of 6. The high jump take-off had holes in it, so Nelson and I moved it onto the center field in an area with good grass. It was slippery but level. I jumped 6' 10". Nelson could hardly believe this. I felt good! These were both national Canadian records. I forgot my form in the shot put and did poorly. The last event is the 400 meters; I hate the 400 or long sprints. I always throw up.

So, I went out very slowly, got far behind, and then realized I just had 200 meters. This really woke me up, so I took off sprinting and ran under 50 seconds better than Rafer Johnson. In fact, scored probably the highest-ever score on the first day of a decathlon. Better the first day than Johnson, the gold standard. I had not eaten all day but still threw up again and again.

I could not eat any dinner that night; I only ate coleslaw and fried foods, which turned my stomach. I ran well in the high hurdles and was at a WR-record pace. I could not get the discus to fly right and performed poorly.

In the pole vault, I borrowed a pole that I could not bend; I had never vaulted before, nor could I get into the proper form of my head. If I could understand the proper form in a field event, I could do it without practice.

On take-off at a higher height (11' 6"), I jammed my toe very hard into the end of my shoe. I took my shoes off, and my toenails were black and blue. I took the safety pin off my number, and Nelson twirled it on the nail until blood squirted out, and the pain was relieved. I taped the nail down so as not to come off. I still had the javelin. Jerry Morrel (Canadian Olympian and Oregon star) vaulted 16'.

After the fiberglass pole, the scale in the pole vault had to be changed. Before, even with an 11' vault, you could get good points, but now, you can hardly get any. He got nearly 1000 points and went ahead of me. I did the javelin in a meet before Trail and threw 191', a great throw. Les Tipton, an Olympian javelin thrower, told me to bury the tip into the point and pick a point out in a cloud so I only see a dot, and it will fly. I planted my high jump shoe, got airborne, and threw it in the air.

Now, my toe was so sore I could hardly plant, and some foreign competitor standing around kept telling me how to throw, which was a big distraction. It made me angry! I could not get it to fly right.

The last event is the 1500 or near a mile. Before the race, both of my legs went into cramps and were very painful. It was very hot; the sun was shining all day, and fumes from the mine were in the air. I had not eaten for two days. I laid down face up, and Nelson sat on my legs and put my sprint shoes on.

When the call came in, I slowly got up and walked with my legs stiff to the starting line. I started slow, and the field got 50 years ahead. After the third lap, in great back pain, I saw only 300 yards to go, took off full speed, and caught the field, but several ran faster; I broke 5 minutes. I scored nearly 7200 points. But the 4200 first day was spectacular! No training and no practice. I had a national US ranking in the decathlon.

That fall, commissioned in the Air Force, I was assigned to Systems Command on a management engineering team. We moved to Los Angeles; I did another decathlon, improving on my shot and discus, moving my score up. I was named to the US team at the Little Olympics in Mexico City, a prelude to the games, testing out the facilities. Still, I had not practiced the pole vault and had to borrow a pole.

Two things happened! First, I found that Bill Toomey and Rick Sloan had entered the meet, so we had three Decathletes but only ten athletes in all. *Would I drop out of the decathlon and enter the long and high jump?*

Next, a Mexican official approached me and said, "Phil, do not worry about the wind. Any jump here in the Olympics will be recorded as a legal jump, so you can go for a world record, and it will be counted."

I went to the long jump pit, and Jesse Owens came over to me and said, "Great jump at Modesto; not sure I could have done that." Although the Modesto all-weather runway was fast, he was on cinders or dirt.

"I heard that you had troubles after Berlin," I said to him.

He opened up, "I was offended by having to race horses and could not get a job. This is the first time I have been honored; they flew me here and treated me well. Mostly, I had no money. Good luck."

Other Black athletes on the 1968 Olympic team called him "Uncle Tom" because he accepted a free ride to the Olympics and had not spoken out against racism. We hugged!

I looked over and saw Igor Ter Ovanejan, the 1964 English Olympic champion Lynn Davies (he told me later, Great Britain or UK, not England, and "I am Welsh") and Jacque Pani, French national champ.

For two years, except for the decathlons, I had not jumped. They called me first in the line-up. I ran easy and in form and jumped 26' 3 ½" and electrified the jumpers. How could this happen? No practice and now near world-class form? This went on to be one of the best meets in history. Igor broke my WR by ¾", Lynn Davies jumper 26' 8" one of his best jumps ever and Pani jumped in the mid 26's. I was fourth, and my subsequent jumps were bad. I lost my form, tried too hard, and went straight up and straight down, out of form and uncoordinated, yet my 26' first jump was spectacular.

Everyone knew I was not here in the open long jump. In the high jump, I made nearly 6' 10" and placed 5th, but all the great jumpers from Russia and Europe were there. I had the best long jump and high jump combination in history.

At higher heights in the high jump, I was out of control. I was strong but distracted by my success, thinking I might win, brushing the bar off at higher heights by stupid errors.

Chapter 16: More Injustice in the 1968 Olympic Trials after Leaving the Decathlon, Thinking about 29' in the Long Jump, Daughter Born

In the decathlon, without a good pole vault, you could not get a good score. Before that, low heights were okay. Learning the pole vault never was my interest; I was always in a technical event, watching someone do it right. For example, in Tokyo, during the games, I watched Valery Brummel's high jump; this changed everything! He approached the bar low, and on his last several strides, he ran with long strides so the center of gravity was low.

Then, on take-off, on the plant, he used his front foot like a pole; with the second to last stride of the power move, his front foot did not bend as American did to spring but stayed straight. While the front leg went up, the take-off leg never left the ground until the front foot was overhead near the bar.

In the US, a jumper would spring down on take-off and then explode up. This created pressure on the take-off leg, which collapsed and became unstable. John Thomas did this and was able to jump 7' 3" by slowing down and not rushing. Hard to do as the bar gets higher; wanting to use more force is counterintuitive. This is what I taught John Louie!

In the pole vault, watching Fred Hansen and Brian jump, they pressed their lower arm straight on the plant and put pressure on the pole to bend. They then lifted their legs up and fell backward in the air, waited for the pole bend, then unfurled while in a good position to vault over catapulted.

Since I could not afford a pole and I had just an hour to work out, the Air Force let me out at 3:30 PM after a full day's work coming in at 7:30 AM; I was short of time. This first jump in Mexico City surprised me. I did it unconsciously, and after the first try, I thought about my form and thought too much, which interfered with my rhythm. Thinking while in flight is a distraction!

Brian's accident may have festered in my mind; I saw others break their pole and get hurt. Brian once lost his balance and came down on the vault box, severely sprained his ankle. On the plant, I felt a pain in my mid back; I used a stiff borrowed pole, but I could not bend the pole.

Doing what Fred Hansen told me of pulling back on the pole and raising feet overhead meant crashing into the pole since it did not bend to the side; the pole was in the way. This messed me up! Later, years later, from X-rays, I had scoliosis as well as a spine that deviated in two directions; I had a herniation in my mid back (fourth thoracic vertebrae).

Thus, this jolt on the plant was dangerous, and I might have created a spinal injury. Unknown then, but the pain on take-off alarmed me.

Later, I found out that weight event throwers and decathletes (perhaps others) took anabolic steroids, and orthopedic surgeons financed the Los Angeles Striders and gave out the anabolic steroids. Many of those I worked out with had been on the Olympic team in 1964, and some others were world record holders. No one told me about these performance enhancers, a well-guarded secret. Other countries did the same but under different national systems. I do not think the coaches or officials knew of this.

Bob Tracy was a coach of the 1967 US national team in Mexico and South America. I met him in Winnipeg in the winter of 1965 when I stayed with his prize athlete, Van Nelson, and his family. I broke the long jump and high jump national records indoors, and as usual for me, I was informed that the Winnipeg meet did not apply to the national organization for a permit. Thus, I did not get the records.

One night on our 1967 trip to Santiago, Chile, Tracy and I went out for a drink in a nightclub; I ordered pisco sours. After a long night, I drank 21 of them, marking each on a paper table covering. Bob said to me, "Let's figure out how far you could jump in Mexico City for the games. Let's start with 27' 5", your first measurement."

"How was the jump?"

"I dropped my feet and landed, standing up and not extending my legs. Since my right leg was 27' 10", let's add 8 inches. This puts us at 28' 6", with no improvement except good form."

"With no practice for two years, you jumped 26' 3 ½". What about altitude and less air resistance? You already know the runway is fast, so let's add 6 inches. This puts us at 29', but you are older and now have better form, not even sure what form you had at Modesto, nor do you remember, I think, the hang form."

I had mastered the double hitch kick, where you run in the air 2 ½ times before landing. Before that, I just hung in the air and, at the last moment, thrust my legs out for the landing.

"You used this in Mexico City. I saw that; let's be conservative and add 4 inches. This puts us at 29' 2 ½"."

This was all recorded on the paper tablecloth, so we went back to the hotel, and the bellhop asked if we wanted girls tonight (it was 3 AM).

Bob said, "Let's do it."

I waited up on the second floor. I was married to Carol and took it seriously. *Would I get a disease, or would I violate my oath?*

Bob had ten kids, so probably his wife shut him off. The girls came, and Bob came running up to find me. I hid behind a wall-length curtain and heard him calling for me. Then, he went downstairs and said he could not find me, and the girls left.

After they left, I said, "I was waiting upstairs."

That fall, Carol became pregnant again with our second child. We packed our bags and drove to South Lake Tahoe for high altitude training and were able to get a three-bedroom apartment which we shared with Pat Traynor, American record holder in Steeplechase; he had two kids, so four kids under three in a three-bedroom apartment.

After Shannon's birth in 1966, I loaded Carol and Shannon into our old 1957 Volkswagen after exiting the hospital. As she ducked in with Shannon in her arms, she turned to me and spoke.

"No one told me about childbirth. I never want to go through this again; it was the worst experience in my life. If someone would have told me how painful this was, I would have never had kids."

When I took her to the hospital weeks before in Tahoe for our second child, she was dreading the labor. I went home, and the phone rang when I got into our apartment.

"Come to the hospital right now."

My mother and I jumped in my car. Carol's mother, Jane, did not stay with Carol. We got off the elevator, and Quincey was rolled out from the delivery room; she came out in ½ hour. Carol was happy, not traumatized like before. Quincey just slipped out. So, between our kids and Pat, one kid or another would wake up, but whose kid?

So, the four of us got up at the sound of any crying. Up and down all night. No sleep for any of us! Shannon was walking at seven months, precocious, and sometimes marched over Pat's kids. His wife was very upset, so there was lots of tension.

One afternoon, Charlie Mays (he was the alternate long jump alternate in 1964) came to our door. The kids were running around, Carol holding Quincey. He had two very large black men with him on each side; I guessed 6' 6" as Charlie was under 6'.

123

"I have come to kick your ass," Mays said menacingly.

His thugs stared at me. I looked around and immediately thought, *The one on the right, I will throw through out the window and settle with the other two.*

They looked out of shape. This was dangerous for the children; the kids were here and there. I walked right through them, and they parted. I opened the door, extended my arm through the open door, and they left. I said nothing! They could see my mood and backed down. I sent Carol back to Seattle with her parents. Moved to a trailer at Echo Summit with Bill Miller, another jumper.

Mays was the alternate in 1964, and I beat him by ¾". He was from Jersey City, and I learned later that Blacks from Jersey City were tough and would get in your face. He was trying to distract me. Although just under an inch when I beat him in 1964, I did not feel him a threat since I was jumping near 27' on each jump since I lost 8". I jumped off the runway and never hit the board. This was not the last of his tricks.

On Monday of the week of the finals, I decided to test my condition. I ran three 200 meters back-to-back at under 22 seconds with little rest. I was not at full speed, but I was sprinting hard. I wanted to see the effect of thin air on the quick runs. I took less rest than when I did this in college. I threw up after the last one and was in pain, which I knew, by experience, would go away in fifteen minutes. I lay in a porta pit; a doctor of the team ran over to me and said we need to test you. He took a urine sample; they were looking for kidney damage due to the altitude. He informed me that I was in danger of kidney damage and I had to rest and take some medicine. The medicine turned my urine purple; he said I needed to rest the final week before the trials, literally bitter medicine to swallow with no training. I needed to work on my steps that week and do short sprints.

Tom Waddell, a decathlete and team physician (who held sick calls every afternoon at 3 PM at Echo Summit) several days before my finals, heard about the pills that prohibited me from practice and came to me.

"Phil, that doctor did not know what he was doing. By taking the sample right after your tough workout, he saw a lot of sentiment floating around in his test tube. If he had waited and had you urinated out your bladder, you would have been normal. You just had a hard workout. I was doing the same. It's good to have a hard workout a week before the trials."

A whole week of step training was wasted before the finals and a bitter medicine.

I was asked to comment about racism in the US that week and agreed to a nationally televised interview on a major network. I knew the subject well from my experiences with Al Pemberton and Bob Flowers and my own fraternity and their "nigger" comments, plus redlining. I talked about this and that we were just a few generations away from slavery. And also that the Whites had a lot to do with hidden racism from slavery and Blacks suffering this constant wound experienced in their lives due to a Jim Crow upbringing.

Sports were far more equal, and these Black athletes were like brothers. It aired nationwide. At that time, if you said racism existed, then this was sedition since it cast a bad light on the US internationally. Not to be spoken!

Several days before the finals, a full Air Force colonel walked up to me and spoke, "Captain Shinnick, if you give another national interview like that, we will pull you out of the Olympic trials and send you to Vietnam or court martial you. Do you understand?"

I did not answer and was shocked because I felt I did not say anything that was untrue and that my comments were reserved.

So, I lost the whole week of sharp training being drugged with a potent kidney medication. How much would it weaken me? I learned the rules. Those who jumped 25' 8" in the preliminary round the day before the finals went to the finals, and I jumped 25' 8" exactly below Boston. I think Boston was second, and Bob Beamon jumped in the low 24 feet near last. This meant Beamon would not get to the finals, but they changed the rules and advanced him.

The night before the final 1968 Olympic trials at South Lake Tahoe, a giant spider came down from the rafters and then jumped down on me. I saw it coming, so I hit my elbows hard on the bed so as to raise it from the bottom sheet. I pulled the sheet from under me with my right arm in one motion and captured the spider in the sheet. I jumped up and uncovered the sheet, but I could not find the spider. I looked all over the room! I wrenched my right shoulder hard. This must have been a dream, but I seemed wide awake. It became a harbinger of what was to come that day.

I had my steps down that morning; I figured that I could jump the Olympic record of 26' 5" and hit 26' 6" and do three consecutive jumps. Everything was to plan! At the games, I would uncork a world record, but here, I just needed to be conservative and make the team. Through the first four rounds, Boston, Beamon, and myself were on the team. I relaxed, but the other jumpers were not doing well, and it did not look good for any of them.

Mays was a mess and barely made the top four, but well behind me and not a threat. He seemed spooked and rattled. I extended my legs out from the bench, sitting as Boston and Beamon were on both sides of me and, appropriately, the three 27' US jumpers on the team. I relaxed!

I happened to look over to my right shoulder and saw Payton Jordan, the head Olympic coach, with his arm around Mays, calming him down. This was a direct violation of the Olympic rules, with no coach on the field and no coaching during the competition; we all knew this!

Mays then jumped ahead of me by several inches; I was flabbergasted. This was wrong, and this injustice deeply affected me. I had two jumps left; I would have to change my plans and go for a world record to make the team. Boston and Beamon were over 27'. They stopped jumping and passed; thus, it was just Mays and me. Now fourth, an alternate, with two jumps to go in the finals.

My steps were on, and I was a veteran, so I knew I would get a good jump, stay in form, and increase my intensity without tension. I was ready for this! I knew what was happening. Mays was a conservative Black, and coaches knew he would not make trouble at the games like the other militant athletes, like John Carlos, Tommie Smith, Lee Evans, and others. This interview became well known, and Jordan was known as a racist in private but glad-handing Blacks in public. The word was out to get me off the team!

1968 Lt USAF Phil Shinnick, jumping in a French National Olympic jersey. South Lake Tahoe Final Olympic Trials

I took off down the runway and stayed within myself on my steps. I felt a new world record coming; I felt thrilled and would get back on the team. The long jump runway was just eight feet from the all-weather track on the right, and trees were between the runway and track, yet 30' from the take-off board, there was a clearing.

Before I ran down the runway, I saw Mays watching me through the trees on the track. I could see he was going to run alongside me, but I was not concerned; the trees blocked him. Five steps from the board through my peripheral vision, Mays was right beside me on the track, a little ahead so I could see him. I uncorked a great jump, which Boston told me was 27' 8", a new world record, but fouled by a hair.

Mays did another dirty deed: it was illegal to harass a fellow competitor. I had one more jump. Same thing, but this time, I would avoid him and gaze to the left. I had a fair jump by avoiding Mays but ended up on the far-left side of the pit while taking off on the right side of the board. Staying right always meant a straight jump and always far; I had corrected this from previous errors of jumping to the left side of the pit, but this time I did not.

From take-off to landing, it was about 27', but they do not measure a direct line, only from a perpendicular. They put a plank board extension over the take-off board to extend to the left side of the board and runway to measure since I shanked the jump left. It was 26' 6". I was off the team!

I went into a deep depression and did not work out for three weeks. At work, I got a call from an Olympic coach that they needed me to jump against the German Olympic team in Flagstaff, Arizona, at altitude. I had to take a small plane to get to Flagstaff, which was ready for me. My gear was in the back, and it was a four-seater. I roomed with Harold Connolly, who knew what had happened at the finals.

On the weekends, I weight-trained with him in his garage in Santa Monica, along with all the other Olympic weight-event athletes. Connolly and I, along with Tom Waddell, were part of the athlete's movement against racism. My competitive gear was missing when I got off the plane, but I saw it was put on the plane; this was more of the same harassment of me. I borrowed some flats and a sweatsuit; I would jump in flats and make the best of it. No bellyaching! I guess I was numb.

Just minutes before my event, someone brought my shoes and uniform out. I did run through my steps once. Usually, I do it a few more times before the event starts. I jumped the high 25's. Very controlled.

Two of the German jumpers surpassed me, so I went inches further to beat them; they then crept ahead of me, so I went a few inches ahead of them, about 26' 4". They equaled that, so I had no choice but to go ahead. I jumped 26' 91/2" while Ralph jumped 27' 4 ¾" ahead of my world record. It was a crummy pit, seemed uphill and the runway was worn, I jumped 26' 9 ½" again, besides Boston, Beamon and myself, the fourth best jump in the US that year and in US history. The German jumpers broke the European record.

One word about altitude! After Mexico City, jumps were listed as at altitude because the idea got around that thin air made jumping easier. From experience, this is just not the case! John Powell surpassed Beamon's record at sea level. Thin air means athletes do not have enough oxygen.

Weather is a big factor; competition and the speed of the runway are real conditions that affect the distance. So, thin air is just one factor among many! Thinking this way seems a fetish, that reality is narrowed down to just one thing obscuring the total circumstances.

After the Mexico Olympics in 1968, I heard from friends who were in the Plaza de las Tres Culturas in Mexico City near the stadium. Just days before the opening ceremonies, there were people protesting against poverty and saying that more should be done for the poor. Snipers were stationed on the roofs of buildings in the plaza and opened fire, killing demonstrators and also a Mexican general with the armed forces. Over a hundred died! This was hushed up!

Even today, the films are restricted due to national security. I wondered whether not being in Mexico City was a way to protect me since I probably would have been in the crowd. This was my nature! I was close to John Carlos in 1967 and competed many times in the same meet with Tommie. Lee Evans was even closer to me; they were my buddies. Nothing makes an athlete more friendly than to see others on the same mission to be the best in the world for all time. A special breed, they felt the same way toward me and understood me.

Chapter 17: Bad Conditions in Miami and Back to Tokyo as Team Captain, Trouble in Airplane Production

Ralph Boston hurt his knee several years after Mexico City, I assume, jumping and high hurdling in most of the indoor and outdoor meets, as well as a long career in three Olympic games and multiple other international meets. He also could pole vault. I always felt that if I had learned the pole vault, he and I would be the best decathletes in the world. He also could high jump 6' 8".

I never tried to beat him. Only twice I did; the rest of the time, we knew that the Olympic games were the only real meet. He did coach my 1969 rival, triple jumper Norm Tate, who had superb form and was also a great sprinter. He beat me by inches several times in Moscow and in the national indoors. I jumped well but had a deep hamstring tear on the insertion, could not sit down, and most nights ached, but with a long warm-up, I could jump well.

Beamon was still outdoors in 1969. He did not jump much indoors. In Miami at the nationals, I had an opening jump that put me in the top two. Beamon was faltering, could not get his steps, and seemed unglued. He rarely looked at me, nor did we ever talk. Yet, when I lined up to jump, he watched, not my jump but where I started, then on his turn, went to my mark and used it.

The runway was hard, as I experienced in San Diego; it was unyielding and tough on the legs and lower back. It threw me off since, before that, it was soft; here, it was hard all the way! I learned something from some big failures at the nationals during my UW graduate school days.

As early national competitions finished, I then felt ready. I thought about it and then decided I was not ready to compete. In Miami, I awoke early and worked out. I heard before Valerie Brummel's world record at Stanford he lifted in the morning, doing full squats at over 300 pounds in the morning. On my first jump, I was ready and did well. So, from then on, I worked out in the morning before a big competition.

Beamon could see that I was jumping well; he was an Olympic champ and now a world record holder. He did what I wanted to do in Mexico: jumped 29′ 2 ½″. I learned from my fellow jumpers firsthand observers that the weather was good. Then, before he jumped, it clouded over, the wind picked up, and it lightly started raining.

The wind reading was 2.0 meters per second, something almost impossible to achieve, exactly legal. I remembered what the official told me in 1967 in Mexico City: all WR jumps in Mexico would count no matter the wind. Added to this was the massacre before the games, and they needed world recognition.

In Miami, Beamon lined up on my mark and took off. I was next to the take-off board. He jumped from his wrong foot and jumped 26′ 10″. Amazing, more than that, impossible! We both were named the top two jumpers to the Americas versus Europe in Dusseldorf later in the summer. I had to first compete in the military championships at CISM. In Miami, I did not try to beat Beamon; the hard surface jolted me. I needed to be cautious!

On my third jump after landing, I felt a pop behind my left knee. Before CISM, the military trained in northern Italy for a week; the same routine I learned after the Cow Palace hamstring pull on the other leg, easy jogging, stretching, and time. I could run at about ¾ speed over the next two weeks but felt vulnerable. I did not compete in CISM, which I had won the previous year. It was cold at night. German doctors urged me to come to Dusseldorf, just ten days away; they had the best doctors, and they wanted me.

My victory in the previous 1968 all-military CISM meet in Athens seemed a repeat of Tokyo; a pole vaulter forgot his tape measure and borrowed my tape before I measured and would not give it back. I then counted 135 steps on the dirt runway by foot, ran through several times, and jumped 25′ on a cold night, once a mistake, twice a fool. I did not panic and stayed under control. I wanted to do well that next fall in Tokyo for the Pan Conference Championship. I had been named to the team. I went home to LA to recover and skipped the US vs. Europe meet.

Back in LA, in the middle of the night, I was a staff duty officer for the command and had the code book by my bed; the phone rang at 3 AM, and a C5A Lockheed test plane blew up in Georgia. I put in the proper code and informed the General in Command of the Space and Missiles System Organization, SAMSO, where I was assigned.

The next day, I was called in by my commanding officer of Air Force System Command, contract management, and given project officer for the reorganization of the Lockheed Georgia oversight division. I felt a similar feeling I had working for Robert Thomas at the UW and Alfred North, whose work I reviewed.

Later, North received the Nobel Prize for economics after ten years of refinement of his earlier work. I felt in control; I knew every single position description in the command since I wrote the book. It took me six weeks to rewrite every single position, and I made an appointment with my commander to present my document. I came into his office, saluted, and gave him the book.

He opened his drawer, put it in, and said, "Captain, we want you to do the same for the F-111 fighter plane at Northrop. Congress is happy with your work."

I did two more of these reorganizations; I was as happy as a pig in the mud since Beamon had set the record so high! I felt no urge to continue this world record quest, but I still thought of the 1972 Olympics in Germany.

I had bad feelings when people, out of kindness, would say we are so sorry for the injustice of your world record. I intensely did not want to be the hard-luck boy, but it seemed to please people that, "Hey, this is just a sport." Something like a jump shot at the buzzer did not count, or a serve over the line.

I trained all summer and was healed by the fall. Hilmer Lodge, the chef de mission of the 1969 Tokyo Pan Conference Championships, was a farmer from the valley and an official who was the San Antonio Relays, Mt. Sac director. This is where I did my second decathlon, elevating me to the Little Olympics in Mexico City in 1967. He asked me to sit next to him for a minute. He brought out a piece of paper for me to sign. I had been elected team captain. It said that athletes should not protest with a raised arm on the victory stand like Carlos and Smith did in 1968 or any other gesture.

"Hilmer, I will sign this if the US officials will stay in the same lodging as the athletes and not get drunk at their banquets."

They were in fancy hotel rooms, and we had small dormitory rooms. He withdrew his document and sort of smiled at me. He was a fair man, like most of the officials in California, doing their job for free and loved our sport. He liked me and knew what I was saying.

Francie Larrieu was a teenager but one of our best US female distance runners; her brother was my teammate on the 1964 Olympic team as a distance runner. She was too young to travel with our team, and her parents were concerned that she would not be old enough to go.

Before, Hilmer had called me and told me this. *Would I take charge of Francie and see to it that she would be protected?* Again, I had a reputation as a straight shooter and a moral person, so I said, "Yes."

I think Ron felt I would take care of his sister and perhaps talk with his parents. The Australians, New Zealanders, and US team had a party after a Kyoto side meet after the Pan Conference games. We had been housed in a hotel with all our rooms on a floor together. We all drank sake.

Milt Sanky, a javelin thrower, carried on his back athletes from room to room and hee hawed like a donkey on all fours. Athletes started to feel the effects of the sake, and most lay on the floor in a comatose state.

One by one, they dropped, bodies everywhere. An Australian pole vaulter got his pole, went outside in his underwear, and ran down the street carrying his pole. That woke us up; it was not that warm, so we went out to watch him.

Team Captain Phil Shinnick accepting the team championship in the 1969 Pan Conference Championship in Tokyo, Japan

Francie was by my side all the time and sat on my lap upstairs in the hotel as protection. Most of the male athletes kept yelling, "Kiss Francie."

Meanwhile, I protected her from these drunk athletes; it seemed to be their mission to get a kiss. They would sneak up behind me and try to get a kiss; I would just push them, and they would fall on the floor, unable to get up.

Francie was honey to these busy bees! I did not really understand why they got so drunk on sake. It seemed pretty light for me, even though I drank a lot, perhaps because of Francie. I was vigilant, and in the end, most people were passed out on the floor; only Tony Sneazwell, the winner of the Helms Award for Best Athlete in Australia, Francie, and I were left. I needed to escort Francie and myself to her room to get some rest.

Luckily, I did because one athlete was waiting for his chance with more than a kiss in mind. I got her to her room and told her to lock her door, not to answer it. I went to bed, got up early, and went for coffee. There was Sneazwell. Tony did not seem to get drunk, like me, but drank as much as everyone else and got up early.

"What's up?" I said.

"What's the fuss?" he replied.

He and I did not have hangovers; the rest of the team were still sleeping when we went upstairs. How to explain these athletes getting so wasted is difficult, but I think all the athletes were happy to have a major competition over. They really liked the friendship and sort of overcame their inhibitions and drank too much. Also, I think they had contests downing the sake-like beer. Happy as pigs in mud and fell asleep or passed out.

The high jump was at night, slightly rainy, cold, and jumping off dirt. Earlier in Tokyo, the high jump conditions were the same as in 1969. I knew the situation well, but it was very slippery!

I saw Thomas and Brumel face off in 1964. Thomas was slipping and sliding, and he finally slowed his approach down and made his third attempt at a low height. One of the all-time come-throughs, then went on to get the silver medal. Brumel was poised and in form. The press called Thomas a failure, and this stuck with him for years. And, of course, when we did peace exchanges together under our organization, Athletes United for Peace, I reminded him always of his come through.

Also, he respected me for my 1965 great high jump performance, beating him at Balboa Stadium. I felt this criticism sullied his enthusiasm for jumping; he admitted this. A silver medal is a failure? Really a perversion, John appreciated my concern for him. Brumel, the next year, 1965, broke the WR at Stanford.

In 1969 Tokyo, I warmed up; I had not jumped for over a year and then only in my two decathlons. I never practiced the high jump. My warm-up was perfect at 6' 6", way over. Since the other jumpers were much better than me, I felt I could not outjump them but could do well and started at 6' 8". Everyone else started lower. I made that height on the first attempt and then the next height. At 7', only one jumper made it, Sneazwell. Others tied me, but I had fewer attempts and fewer misses, so I got the silver.

In the 4 x 400 relay, I saw before we left in California at a meet that Jim Frey, our sprinter, was in bad form and out of shape, so I told the coaches he could not run the relay. They went against my advice and put him last, a big mistake. I ran second, and we were in the lead before he got the baton.

We got third! Should have won, but he apologized and said he would do better in the open events. He did! I wondered how he could improve so much, but I think his failure somehow energized him. I wanted to get first. Based on his bad pre-meet shape, why was he on the team? I thought they wanted a White sprinter.

I had two medals and wanted a third medal in the long jump. Esther Chacon, part of my Air Force management engineering team in LA, urged me to see her daughter in Tachikawa at an Air Force base, about a 30-minute train ride south of Tokyo. I promised her.

The only time I could see her daughter was to get up early, take a train, and then come back before the evening long jump. I found her house on the Air Force base since I had a military ID to get through the gate. She had a small apartment, and one of my friends, Lt. Roger Macur, from my work, had dated her, so I vaguely knew her.

Her first comment was, "I have a boyfriend."

I was not sure what that meant since I was married and on a mission for her mother. Esther just would not take no for an answer for me to visit her. I had nothing in common with her daughter, and she sat on the far side of her living room. She stayed as far away from me as possible. I felt offended; I had no personal interest in her! I laid down on her short couch and then fell asleep, missing my train back to Tokyo.

I asked her to drive me to the meet, and she said blatantly, "No."

I insisted, and finally, after a long delay, she drove me. However, it was in a very small car, and my knees were literally on my chest. I felt very uncomfortable with her!

Because of the delay, I made it back with just enough time to get my gear and do a short warm-up. I jumped 25' with stiff legs, a condition from my high jumping and sprinting the night before, and the small car. The other jumpers inched up on me, and several inches separated the top four jumpers; I got fourth.

This episode haunted me for years, and I finally decided that fulfilling a promise should not mean getting defeated. I have always been a man of my word, but this was over the hill; I suffered for many years from this!

Chapter 18: Nature's Injuries through Rough Conditions, Africa, Going for a Ph.D., New Approach to Training, Getting the American Record, Meeting Ernest Becker and Social Protests

Kyoto had similar conditions as Tokyo: cold and rainy, yet the take-off for the high jump wasn't just slippery. It was also soft. On take-off, I froze on the plant as my foot dug down deep, then slid and stopped; I could jump 6' 6" this way.

At 6' 8", I did the same thing, but my take-off foot slipped just as my front foot was above the bar, causing my heel to come right down on the wooden crossbar, a karate chop-like. The bar hit the porta pit and split in two, right on my Achilles heel. I then long jumped, and in the same muddy condition, I went slow and got a fair jump, but not that far. In my next jump, I increased my speed halfway down the runway, my opposite hamstring cramped and torn.

Earlier, on a 1968 goodwill tour of Africa (my booby prize for what happened in the trials), in Mogadishu, Somalia, in the high jump, the pit was sand, the take-off sand. I learned the Kyoto technique of freezing and then releasing from these conditions, and I could barely get over 6'. I decided to wait till a higher height while the other jumpers exhausted themselves and missed; a US official came onto the field and asked why I was not jumping. I responded this was dangerous and could cause an injury. He implored me to compete.

I said, "No, not good for me!"

He insisted that it could ensure better public relations. I relented; the bar, instead of going up two inches, only one inch, first set at 5' 9". This meant jump after jump, landing into the sand at ground level. This hurt my back. An African won at 6' 2" since by

140

then I was hurt. Still, I competed in the 100-meter race, ran two heats, and got a fast time in the sand. At the start, if you go hard, you slip, running like you are on ice.

Lieutenant Phil Shinnick Coaching Somalian Athletes 1968

At the University of Dar Es Salaam, I felt I needed, like up at Tahoe, to test the elements. At high noon at the equator, the track was edged by the jungle, and lions periodically came onto the track. Many students sat on the field. Secretly, I wanted to show these students what a real athlete could do; a practice session was needed. I ran 10, not three as in Tahoe, 200 meters back-to-back, but here I just waited until the nausea went away. I had been seasoned to heat by bucking 10 hours a day, bales all day all summer, and approximate heat.

After I did this over the next years into 1969 and up to Kyoto, I didn't train that much. I think the heat permeated my very center, and this lasted. I had a great Air Force job (so happy to use my brain) and two kids who never seemed to sleep much at night for 5 years. I decided to be a psychologist and took night courses at UCLA and graduate school at Pepperdine. This prepared me to enter the University of California at Berkeley for a Ph.D.

In 1971, the Air Force gave me full-time off for training. From 1967 to 1970, I trained about 45 minutes a day and, on weekends, lifted weights with Connolly in his garage. A history of psychology course required an important historical paper. I picked unconsciousness and consciousness. I felt my aesthetic life at the UW was all about breaking my unconscious habits, blocking pain, desires, and tendencies that distracted me from fully being human and present.

I read Kant, Freud, Hegel, Descartes, and other historical philosophers who addressed this issue. I got an A plus; this awakened me and changed my life, even now, as I am a part of the Foundation of Mind (top scientists in the world) on consciousness. I wrote my UC dissertation in social psychology.

Also, in 1971, while training full-time, I had classes in Berkeley, so I drove up the valley each Sunday night and came home Tuesday midday for two classes. The Air Force put me on full-time training for the 1972 Olympic games; that summer, we moved to Berkeley, my last year in service.

Before I left, my commanding officer put me in charge of the annual commander's briefing at headquarters, arranging all the lodging and programs, but I also had orders to train to bring honor to the Air Force.

My commanding officer was disappointed. Bonne Wilder, my young secretary, asked me to introduce several of her LA friends,

Kathleen Soliah and Jim Kilgore (later, they joined the SLA above-ground organization and were involved with protecting Patty Hearst underground since the government was out to kill her like her comrades) who wanted to move to Berkeley and join community organizing groups. I arranged for them to meet with Jack Scott, who had a Berkeley Ph.D. and served on my oral committee, who had a house in Oakland near the Black Panthers headquarters.

I had X-rays of my lower back in LA after my 1968 African trip; the diagnosis was advanced arthritis in both hips and no treatment except taking 8 aspirins a day for life, yet with a long warm-up, I was okay, just in pain a lot but no new news for me.

My career was mostly pain and suffering. With no time to go to UCLA for training, I trained many days on the cement of the Air Force station. I could not use the training room at UCLA. I came in one day and took a small chunk of ice out of the huge refrigerated pile. A trainer came in and treated me rudely; he was obnoxious, overbearing, and officious.

"Get out of here; that ice is for football player's injuries."

So, I never went back, and I did not want to cause trouble for Jim Bush, the UCLA coach who invited me to train there. So, treating my injuries there was out.

Yet, my body was a wreck! I started to take dance classes in LA with Raquel Welch, dancers, and actors. Pure humiliation! I was tight and a mess, but I suffered through these classes and started to learn yoga. I got better. Still, practice it.

I devised a training plan in Berkeley with three variables for high performance: endurance, speed, and strength. Endurance was uphill running. Power was intense weight lifting with heavy weights with perfect form and low repetition. Speed was sprinting all out on a track. The third day is rest. Each day, depending on weather, mood, and outside pressure, I switched the sequence. Three different things. I ran Strawberry Canyon above the UC stadium up to the Lawrence Radiation Lab, uphill for several miles, then sprinted downhill.

The next day, I had to lift weights, sprint, and then a day off, rotating according to weather, stress, and mood. I stopped all these monster workouts, like at Tahoe or Dar Es Salaam. I wondered whether this was an extension of some sort of punishment from my Catholic discipline, to suffer pain and dedicate this suffering to those in the world in pain and what Christ went through to be more Christ-like.

Buddhists separate pain from suffering; pain is a part of sport, but suffering for me came from my Christian religion. I tried to stop the suffering that I created. Enough was enough! I stopped all these.

In LA, Carol and I took the girls to church each Sunday, and one day, we heard a priest talking *against* open housing while quoting a higher-up bishop or cardinal. This was a defining moment; my faith dissolved instead of uplifting me, as with Alfred North at UW or my consciousness paper. It caused me to rethink my strict Catholic orientation.

In fact, we stopped going to church; this was White Supremacy and, to me, a sin! I have never looked back, but I still read St. Augustine, Buber, Bonhoeffer, Harvey Cox, Hans Kung, and liberation theology. I became ecumenical. To me, it is a wonder that in one day, all my orientation changed. How could anyone turn their back on Black or indigenous people?

Dr. Jack Scott became athletic director and head of PE at Oberlin. After Oberlin, Jack Scott served on the medical staff of four Olympic games. Through his knowledge of sports medicine, he treated key Olympians such as marathoners Joan Benoit to championships and Maria Mutola to a world record in the 800 meters. Ms. Benoit, four days before the Olympic games in 1984, could not walk, and Dr. Scott single-handedly nourished her back to health for a gold medal.

In 2003, through American approval, I felt the door open for me. Lamine Diack was indicted for corruption by French authorities that year, and his son Papa was under investigation for accepting several million under the table.

Chapter 19: Finding a Way for World Record Approval, Training for the 1972 Olympic Team, Daughter Getting Hurt, Learning Resistance

Why did I do this monster workout in Africa, become monk-like (I read too many of Thomas Merton books) in college, deny myself what I wanted, try to reshape my psyche, break habits, try to outmatch everyone in workouts, want to study my jumping, bad runways and lack of meet conditions?

Things became harder, and I doubted my path mentally, but I still trained. However, another world record leap seemed remote due to what I was experiencing. I chose this path and could not leave or abandon it, no matter my doubts.

Still, I did not understand what happened to my world record jump and why discrediting it. I knew that glory passes, and victory forgets fame over time, but a world record is not a won meet or like an Olympic gold medal, which happens twenty-five times each century, every four years. It is far more enduring. I had to find out what had happened!

All became clearer when I called my old friend Primo Nebiolo, elevated to President of the International Amateur Athletic Federation, IAAF. He said the US had never submitted a world record application form after approval. Nebiolo told me to contact Richard Hyman, editor of the world record book.

Hyman told me that since the US federation did not have two wind instruments, the current rule could not be enforced. The US federation was not in compliance because it did not have two wind gauges (these were not available through the federation or IAAF) due to the scarcity of instruments.

Also, this requires a second wind gauge official. My jump, according to Hyman, came under the old 1939 rule; this was more stringent and required 7 meeting officials to agree and support the jump. This had already happened, so now, an avenue had been opened. This took a decade!

I ethically maintained a path of goodness but was seemingly punished in the Tokyo Olympics. I was being humiliated, suffering almost every kind of injury: brain concussions, cracked metatarsals, pulled hamstring, pinched nerves in my back, migraines, sinus infections, and stomach upset. I didn't have any knowledgeable coach, kids that would not sleep, not a good rest at night in years, and political backlash over common sense racial truths, peace tendencies, and socialist/communist identification but broke with little money living in Richmond, California in subsidized housing.

Nevertheless, I was happy to be in graduate school; I was where I wanted to be. I felt at home in Cal; I met many athletes and students who thought like me and were politically active. I had time to organize antiwar races, get anti-nuclear proliferation support, and talk about prohibiting performance-enhancing drugs for athletes. I was given the best intellectual books and time to study without many classes. The professors knew I was self-motivated and needed little guidance.

The campus was under siege; the police and activists rode around in flatbed trucks, the activists up to mischief and the police trying to find them. The harbor had war materials to be shipped out to the war, and small boats protested and blocked their departure. The police put barriers up around campus, so I liked jumping the barriers to see my advisors.

People talk about politics all the time! I spent my time organizing political events, training, reading, and creating a vision of sports based on what was bad. Negate the negation, meaning what is better, is not here, but by making clear the contradictions between what is bad and what needs to be done, it would evolve. I had visions of where to go by reading Teilhard de Chardin (the Omega point of humanity evolving together) in college and now Henri Saint-Simon Simon, Thorstein Veblen, Robert Owen, Fourier, Marx and Engels, and Mao.

Still, I wanted redemption from my suffering in sports by not getting a chance to perform at the 1968 Mexican Olympics. The pain I can take is different. There were no world championships. Boston and Beamon were out. Boston had a bad knee. Beamon pulled his hamstring and never jumped over 27'. He was playing basketball at Adelphi, and now it was my turn and time.

Norman Tate had been jumping well in the large 60s, but in the early 70s, he was not there. Now was my chance to get to Munich; I could not think about winning a gold medal, which would be a distraction (only getting the chance to compete). Now, I have worked on hitting the board and perfecting my approach and speed while healing my injuries by not competing, staying uninjured, and waiting for more than a year. I just needed to get into the finals of the 1972 Olympics.

I did not compete during the Berkeley years except to qualify for the Olympic trials in the spring of 1972; I needed to pass my written exams and orals and then write a dissertation. I wanted to be a professor, and my advisors wanted me to become a university president since I was trained in systems theory (in the Air Force) and had a master's in organizational behavior. From my case studies, I found these positions led to heart attacks and bad health since they had responsibility for things they could not control. I wanted to be a professor.

Tom Tellez, an assistant coach at UCLA, wanted me to extend my approach from 130' to 190', which I practiced for several months. I worked on my approach every day and speed work. I stopped my grinding 200s or 300s, which was very exhausting. However,

I had to be ready 12 months a year, every day, to jump. Finally, with a long approach, I could come off the board with months of practice, as if to jump, but not finish; the back of my knee popped on a trial jump in practice. This speed put too much pressure on my take-off leg, and my body could not handle this level of speed, so I went back to a shorter approach.

Rainer Stenius, a Finnish jumper, tested Boston, Beamon, and myself for speed by setting up sensors on the runway at various points. My speed on the runway was the fastest, but Beamon and Boston were jumping consistently further in minor meets (except in the trials), and I had a hard time controlling my speed. I needed to slow down to go further.

I wrote down all my workouts and kept track of running times, weights lifted, and heartbeat upon raising; if my heart rate went up in the morning, then fatigue showed, so I rested. Other things were important: coldness, hot, rain, wind, my stress, track conditions, and amount of rest.

At first, at Berkeley, I trained with the Cal track team, but like most college kids, they worked out too hard, plus they tried to challenge me. One day, we did sprints off the turn, and after the 10th fast one, I let up; this was way too much for me, unnecessary.

As I let up, the athlete in front of me pulled his hamstring muscle. I watched it pop from behind. The Cal track spooked me; I had never before competed with athletes in practice (at the UW, the coach always had me run alone) with other athletes. It was worthless, and it meant nothing.

At UCLA, I ran speed times with other athletes at the same pace. We never competed against each other but ran side by side in unison. I never went back to the Cal track for practice after that. I found a fast all-weather track at Contra Costa Junior College just north of Richmond, a 20-minute drive. I trained alone, and no one was on the track when I was there.

My workout was to jog several miles easily, do ten wind sprints in bare feet on the grass infield, do a set of yoga asanas, go through my steps on the runway 6 times (I had never done this consistently), and then run on the track.

On the track, I did a timed 150 under 15, which is fast; I got this down to 13.5, which is more than world-class speed. I did this only once or, if the weather was good, twice. I liked to do an endurance workout the next day, take a day off, and then, if I was still sore again, do an endurance workout after the day off.

When there is good weather, or my outside stress is low, I would take a day off and then sprint again, the same with weightlifting. If there is bad weather, then lift weights, take a day off, and lift again. So, each day, I could change my workout according to mood and conditions.

One day, after studies and class, I came back to our Richmond crescent, three-bedroom townhouse. It was subsidized but very nice, in a semicircle, but no one was home; the neighbor said that my daughter Quincey had fallen out of the second-story window and was in the hospital near my training site. I jumped in my car; the California highway was packed going north but still going 70 mph.

Just the thought of Quincey being hurt froze me; my peripheral vision receded, and all I could see was a dot far off. I thought If it all became black, then I would pass out and, at 70 mph, would crash. I knew that scene from high school. I thought, *Here I am, going to see my daughter and kill myself on the highway by passing out.*

I became one pointed in the far-off dot of light. If I captured it, I could bring myself out of it. After some time, it expanded; luckily, all the cars stayed in line during my panic about losing my daughter.

At the hospital, Quincey was in a crib with a plastic bubble overhead. They had a rocking chair nearby. I lifted her out of the crib and put her on my lap, and she snuggled up to me as if nothing was wrong. On the way home, I learned she had pushed on a window screen that came loose while Carol was in the same bedroom and fell headfirst into the garden outside.

Quincey, the age she fell out of a window

They found her in a wooden box, 18" x 18" x 18", with a wooden stake in the middle. She was curled around the stake in this small box. Figure that one out!

Just a month before, my other daughter Shannon had been attacked by a bratty neighbor boy who got a brick and threw it at her face. All bruised up and created a bone spur on her facial bone, which I massaged for weeks and then dissolved. My three workouts, endurance, speed, and strength, were on different days with a fourth day off; days of the week did not matter.

Finally, I was not beating myself up and healing. I did enter two sprint races, once in the fall and then one in the spring. The Bay

Area had the Olympic champ James Hines, the fastest sprinter in the world, and local Willie Williams tied the world record, and many were near that, which is a great tradition.

That 1971 fall, south of SF on a track near the Bay, there must have been 20 sprinters from all over the Bay. Everyone wanted a fast time; I was the only White sprinter. We ran in heat. I ran 6.2 for 60 (for the track, this was good) and was far ahead of anyone else. I could see these young sprinters were nervous about my presence.

In the spring, I ran at San Francisco State, which had a terrible hard surface track, and all the best sprinters were in one heat. I ran 9.5 on this terrible track, won by a big margin, and was sore for weeks; I stopped competing in the sprints, which was too risky.

On New Year's Eve in late 1960, I was in Ernest Becker's apartment near the SF State campus, where he had gotten the Pulitzer prize for his book *Denial of Death*. At Cal, Becker was the most popular teacher; the auditorium was full when he spoke, and outside loudspeakers broadcasted to students sitting and gathering around the building.

The higher-ups were afraid of him, fear of another free speech movement, student unrest, and student protests, which haunted them. They let him go, but SF State hired him. The SF State president called in the police to quell student protests over ethnic studies issues. Becker said he would not go on campus when the campus was under police occupation, so he asked all his students to come to his apartment for his teaching.

They all liked that the president fired him. He got a professorship at Simon Fraser in Canada. When he got there, the students went on strike over the Vietnam War, and they asked professors to support their protest. He had had enough of these strikes, and Canada was not at war; only the US was, so he went on campus.

He needed to feed his family; he had several kids. The students harassed him and called him a scab; this had a very bad effect on him, as he had already been in two universities and had been fired for his politicking.

My discussion with him that night was that if you are going into the hot frying pan, you must learn to create a calm body (even learn yoga). Injustice harms the body if one does not learn how to deal with it.

This was a harmful influence on the body. He was not an athlete, so I think he thought this was something foreign to him and strange; he died of cancer of the stomach just a year or so after going to Canada. Obviously, to me, that is where his tension went. I warned him of that and felt a great tragedy—a brilliant life cut short by not learning how to overcome tension inside the body protecting his life. It got to him!

Chapter 20: Nursing an Injury, Carol Tortured by Nude Pole Dancer Saying Baton Twirling Sexist, An Institute to Publish Sport Stories, Radical Athletes

Carl Lewis used this long approach at 180′ and trained with Tom Tellez, his new coach at Houston. He won gold medals in sprints and long jumps. My injuries in Kyoto, later in the spring of 1970, not having time to work out on the good UCLA new tartan track and instead making wind sprints on the cement at the LA AF Station, aggravated my Kyoto-hurt Achilles.

In Kyoto, after my Achilles injury, the next day, I went to a Kyoto Japanese drug store and explained my injury. She watched my motion of what had happened. She gave me a clay-like substance and material to build a cast. I spread this clay over my heel and Achilles and then wrapped the gauze around my ankle and added some water, but shortly, it became hard. I wore this cast for several days, and like a miracle, the swelling went down, and I had no problems until that 1970 spring. I was named to a team to go to Martinique, an island in the Caribbean.

I went to Dr. Rosenfeld, a doctor for the SC Striders, on Monday. He entered the room and said he had been watching my career and had one arm behind his back. He told me to show me where it hurt, felt the area with one hand, then his other arm came out with a needle, and he injected cortisone in the area.

A nurse came in and put a knee-down cast on my right leg, then said, "Take it off before you get on the plane." I took it off Friday, no pain.

Twenty years later, my Achilles swelled up, and it took me ten years to heal it.

In Martinique, the conditions were primitive. Otis Burrell came as another high jumper and was missing at low heights. It was clear

I would beat him, and I noticed he was jumping in his flats, his spikes were lost, and he was the national champion. He beat me in the 1965 nationals by 1", 6' 11" to 7'. I did not like this; he was sitting, waiting for his turn, so I gave him my left jumping shoe, and he went on to beat me. Who wants to beat someone under unfair conditions?

This new routine meant I could sprint one day, rest a day, and sprint again. The same was true with weightlifting (also endurance running): lift, rest, then lift again. In this way, big improvements would be made in the three areas: endurance, speed, and power. I decided not to do what I was doing with Russ Hodge at UCLA: lift for three hours on Sundays, lots of repetitions on a ram rack at an angle with weights on slides. We could lift 3 or 4 hundred pounds and do three sets of 15 or 25. Also, bench pressing with heavy weights and spotters, I could do 300, Russ 450.

Now, in 1971, I lifted heavy weights with just one or two repetitions and only total body lifts like the deadlift, clean and jerks (lifting an Olympic bar from the floor up to the chest), and one-legged step-ups onto a bench. No squats. I had no spotters.

After the cleans, by getting the bar up to my shoulders in front (the weight rested on my chest with elbows up), I went to bench pressing, then did step-ups one leg at a time, warming up with one lift at lower weights.

After some months, as I became stronger, I did 300 on a clean, and then I did one rep with one leg on a step up for each leg with perfect balance. Each day, either running uphill or sprinting and weightlifting, I tried to concentrate completely at each moment, training my mind and body not to be distracted during workouts, as if in competition.

The war in Vietnam had supply ships in the Bay harbor, and demonstrators, in small boats, were trying to block passage.

Downtown, there were strip joints everywhere, a sexual revolution brewed, pornography, pole dancing, and a large gay population.

Carol became a target for radical feminist women; baton twirling and cheerleading were seen as sexist. She was egged by Paul Hock (who called cheerleaders and baton twirlers sexist and had a Ph.D. in Physics from Brown at 19 and a Ph.D. from the London School of Economics) in his book *Rip Off the Big Game, The Exploitation of Sport by the Power Elite*. He also brought this manuscript to the Institute for the Study of Sport and Society, set up by progressive athletes as a clearing house for athletic abuse, racial and sex discrimination, and drug abuse.

A meeting was called to discuss Carol's baton twirling and the sexist nature of this art; we met in our low-income Richmond Crescent townhouse. The women roundly condemned her pedantically, going on and on, running a rap on her to put her down. I did not know what to say since, from a larger picture, this may be true, but women at that time could not participate in sports, and this was the only way athletes like Carol could participate in athletics. She trained hard like any athlete.

In Seattle, she was loved, respected, and honored for her skill. Carol was emotionally hurt and disgusted; she was making money for our family by teaching high school girls the art.

These women criticizing her made their money by pole dancing nude in the city. Other radicals we met were putting cement in the toilets of banks and crazy glue in their locks. Their philosophy was "Fuck the System." Meanwhile, Carol and I were accomplished. In Seattle, we held press conferences on racial and political issues. I saw them as anarchists with anger toward the system but not part of it.

Jay Weiner, a teenage precocious sportswriter, came to our institute and compiled press clippings from around the US, arranged into two office file cabinets. In 1968, Harry Edwards, a weight man at San Jose, influenced athletes at SJS like Tommie Smith, Lee Evans, and John Carlos on Black power. He came in one day and, for a week, took the file cabinet of clippings Weiner had collected and wrote his Ph.D. dissertation at Cal from these files. We published books from firsthand accounts of abuse.

Dave Meggyesy, a seven-year linebacker for St. Louis, wrote the most popular book with Jack Scott's help, *Out of Their League.* Meggyesy, in the late 60s, kneeled before a game in solidarity for racial discrimination and the next year was benched and then let go a year later. Jack, Jay, and Mikki, Jack's wife, did the day-to-day business; I had a desk at the institute in Oakland near the Black Panther's headquarters.

Two things caused me to move out: Carole King was at a concert in Berkeley, and Jack paid for my ticket since Carol and I had no money. I was in line behind Jack at the outside entrance. He had my ticket, and as we got closer to the gate, he still had not given me the ticket. I felt like a beggar! I lingered, falling back in line. I stopped, then decided to turn back, deeply hurt by what I thought was a sadistic gesture. Jack confirmed this by turning around at the last minute (I fell back ten people) to give me the ticket and smiled in a mischievous way.

Jack and I later decided what we would say at a press conference the next day, and he scheduled the press conference for when I would not be there. When I got there, he told me what he said, which was different from what we agreed upon. He said that he and Mikki had stayed up all night discussing this and decided to change it. Why was I not there with them? They did not understand that every day at 4:30 PM, I went home to have dinner with Carol and put the girls to bed and never went out at night. All these radicals did not have kids except Dave Meggyesy.

Athletes started to come to Berkeley. Chip Oliver was an Oakland linebacker, George Sauer, Joe Namath's go-to end, and an intellectual like Dave. The institute published *High for the Game* by Chip and then *Meat on the Hoof* by Gary Shaw on Texas football, as well as another book on boxing.

We all had Thanksgiving together. Dave's kids and mine ran around the house chasing each other, up and down, while sliding down the banister. Chip had two joints in his mouth at once and seemed to inhale both of them. I watched both embers burn to the end. How could he get that much in his lungs? He had joined a Berkeley commune and given all his money to them; all the girls liked and adored him, and he seemed happy. We had a huge turkey. I was to give the portions out. I thought it was cool at first.

Dave came up to me with a plate in hand and seemed mighty hungry. "Give me a hunk."

I tore off a piece with my bare hands; one by one, they stood in line, and I ripped the turkey apart. When I served, everyone would say, "Alright." Lots of hooting and shouting high energy.

One time, Dave, Chip, and I went to Harbin Hot Springs, which was just a hot pool in a wooden shed. An eye was painted in the corner, outside a wood railing, and below a creek with rocks some 150' down.

In the pool (about 4' deep), Chip did the fire breath, forced air out through the nostril, making a snorting sound, rapid, to me a very long time, 200 hundred snorts. Then, he slowed it down for three breaths, and in the center of exhalation and inhalation, he stopped his breath, looked at the eye in the corner, put his arms out, and fell backward in the hot pool, head back.

We waited for what seemed to be five minutes, and up Chip rose with arms out and slowly breathed. He got out of the pool, so we went outside. He climbed up on the railing, which was about 4 inches wide, right over the abyss below of rocks and water. He faced the abyss and then extended his chest; he did his breathing with eyes closed. Head back, like a bow (wow), he did not move for five minutes. Chip was in another space. Once, Dave left for several days and had a couple of lids in his attic. When he returned, Chip had smoked it all.

On the way back to town, he promised someone that he would help dig out the dirt to put up some stairs, which was a big job, so we went to it. The dirt flew, and Chip was like a tornado; I had never seen anyone work so fast. We seemed to finish in minutes, and Chip turned to me, dirt all over him, wide-eyed with a shit-ass grin on his face; he had taken mescaline.

Hanging out with these star progressive athletes, locals from Cal athletics, and community organizers has helped me develop my organizing and political skills. Yet I was different; they did not have skin in the system, so they were trying to beat down the system. I had been inside and had contacts and respect that they did not have. Yet still, I enjoyed their rantings, but I spread out into radio, film, congressional support, and local college teaching.

Chapter 21: My Brother Nelson Combat Helicopter Pilot Home from Vietnam, Tom Waddell and the Gay Games, Steroids in Sport, Founding a Track Club

One of my Olympic teammates, Mike Manley, a steeplechaser, saw me at a meet. He said when he was in Marine officer training camp and running a long race over sand, which was physically hard. Near the finish, he looked over to see someone next to him. Surprised, he said, "Who are you?"

He said, "Shinnick."

Mike then said, without hesitation, "No wonder you are Phil's brother."

Manley and my brother became good friends. Later, my brother Nelson just came back from Vietnam and visited me in the Bay Area.

I mentioned the Manely story to him, and he said, "I set the All Marine obstacle course record. They had a 6' or so high wall that you had to pull yourself over; everyone stopped to get over, so I ran at it, jumped up, put my foot halfway up the wall, and vaulted over."

That afternoon, we drove to the countryside, parked the car, and walked out onto a field; the ground had just been turned over and was uneven. I had a Colombian joint, which a friend gave me while sitting on the ground, and we shared it. I do not think he had ever smoked a joint.

Once, I tried it in college, but I waited five years later until after I was out of the Air Force to smoke anything. I asked why he was able to come back alive, but most of his fellow pilots did not make it. He said that he listened to the radio and heard when a copter had been shot down at what altitude. His topographical map had all the hills numbered, so he knew the exact location of where not to fly back to the base.

From this map, he memorized all the hills, where the guns were stationed, and altitude. If he came under fire anyway, then he pulled the copter stirring lever hard to the right to make it go sideways, which gave the illusion that he was flying straight. In this way, they always shot in front of him. He said the copters rattled and seemed to fall apart but didn't break up. I think our work on our grandfather's farm, with heavy machines at 14, gave him a good sense of navigation. Missiles from aircraft carriers regularly whizzed by overheard and to the side from behind.

On the first day on duty, he went to the ready room and saw red (which he knew to be blood) on the floor. Just a day before, the Vietcong had gotten into the base and killed all the pilots. He tried to figure out how they got onto the base. So, the next day, he flew back along the river, which flowed through the base, about three feet above the water, and saw the enemy underwater with reed straws.

One jumped up out of the water to shoot him, but his gunman in the back killed him first. He said he once crashed upside down in a river, then swam ashore, ran as fast as he could back to the base two miles away, and shot anything that moved.

He spoke about one mission. He was heading back to the base to refuel and get more ammunition when he heard a call over the radio that Marines were pinned down in the jungle and needed rescue. He headed to that location and attacked, turning on a siren of his Huey, which could wake the dead with a blood-curdling noise. They didn't fire at him, and the transport behind him rescued all the Marines.

After recounting this, he suddenly jumped up and started to run back to the car at full speed. He had a three-yard head start. I caught up next to him and said, "Where are you going?"

He said he needed to get back to the ready room. I could not pass him; he was hell on wheels, perhaps running back to the base in his mind after his crash. He laid down in the back of the car and said, "When is this going to get over? I do not like what I see."

He said that he was responsible for deaths up in the hundreds from his rockets and napalm. When I stayed overnight with him, he yelled and screamed in his sleep. This never left him! He did well with the General phone company for 15 years, then the next 20 years, his nightmares spread to the days, and his whole being suffered until his death.

At that time, Tom Waddell, MD, the decathlon Olympian, came from the city over the Oakland bridge once a week. He worked as an emergency physician and later became a head physician at SF General. He, Jack Scott, and I discussed what was to be done in this historical phase in athletics and which direction the Institute for the Study of Sport and Society we formed should follow. He had just competed in Hawaii in the high jump.

On take-off, he ripped his quadricep completely from the insertion, pulled it back down, taped it up, and flew back to SF to have it sewn back together. I competed against him in the military championships in San Jose in June 1968. I was in top shape, jumping around 26′ early in the season; he jumped 21′ and out of shape.

He had been a preventive physician in the Army, like me, was threatened with a court martial for his peace activities the previous spring in the Army by showing a Graham Green film on base (for me, this came after a national television interview I did up at South Lake Tahoe in September on racism the week before the final Olympic trials).

Instead, the Army gave him time off to make the Olympic team in the decathlon. He had his eye on me throughout the meet. I did not know who he was, but he looked like an athlete. Before 1968, when the finals came at Echo Summit in Tahoe, he was jumping 24' and high jumping over 6' 6", all in 2 ½ months. He was 6th in the Olympic games in the decathlon and did five personal bests.

Left. 1968 Tom Waddell practicing at South Lake Tahoe

In 1969, I was chosen to compete, and Tom became the team physician for a dual meet between the US and the Soviets in Moscow. We were seldom apart; he was a progressive athlete and an intellectual.

So, we spent our time in art galleries and museums. I told him my secret about the long jump take-off, which he tried in Kiel, Germany. He took off with great form and great lift from the board but broke his back by compressing a discus. He said he tried to do what I told him but did not have the back strength. He took anabolic steroids after the Army released him for training. He felt this was a natural thing to do and saw no ethical concerns; for me, this was a fly in the ointment. Jack wrote a history of performance-enhancing drugs in all sports for the *New York Times Magazine*, where he quoted Bill Toomey's admission in a press interview by Ira Berkow taking anabolic steroids.

Jack also had firsthand knowledge of amphetamine use in the 400 and in practice when he was a freshman at Stanford and Bill was training there. Toomey became the Olympic champion and, with Russ Hodge, later set the world record. Bill knew I was close to Jack, so our relationship was strained and never repaired. Bob Lipsyte from the *NY Times* was a journalist writer who interviewed Jack and wrote his obituary for the Times. But to me, a close friend.

Later, in 2010, I complained bitterly to Bob about steroid use (at the Svitz in Lower Manhattan).

He just said, "Why didn't you take them? There is no testing, except in big competitions, and many ways to beat the system. All the countries are using them, so why such a big fuss?"

Toomey was not alone, and this was normal during that period.

Yes, why the big fuss? Why bring this up? If I took steroids and broke the world record, then what could I say about this, that it was the steroids that did it? Athletes like Toomey, who was a 23' long jumper (to 26') and a 6' 2" high jumper (to 6' 8"), are a big advantage.

Also, in Tom's case, out of shape, each week for $25, I drove to Cal State Hayward under a National Institute of Mental Health grant to lecture by video about performance-enhancing drugs. I organized and testified before a Senate hearing with Birch Bayh for the publication of the *Improper and Proper Use of Drugs Among Athletes*.

I testified before a UNESCO international sports conference and said drug use was perverting the sports culture and undermining hard work and the essence of sport. I was named an ambassador of UNESCO; then, I went to Cuba to the *International Tribunal*, which was held at the International Youth Festival. I wrote for educational journals on performance and restorative drugs, which became one of my life's works. I insisted that testing had to be done while training. One could take, then get strong, and then stop for several months.

Taking steroids does not make you strong; you have to train hard. Toomey was a hard worker and benefited from this, and he complained to me that I did not give him credit. However, I did see training at UCLA with him in a short time period. His bench press went from nearly 220 to over 300 in weeks taking them. He worked very hard, as did Tom Waddell.

Tom became an advocate of gay men doing sports, joined a gay bowling league, and then had the idea of a "Gay Olympics," which he organized with others, but the US Olympic committee sued him personally. I drove to San Francisco to see him before he died of AIDS. He complained that a treatment for AIDS could be developed; he was a specialist in tropical and rare viruses, but he would not see that and would die.

As a matter of fact, days before he died, he called me on the phone and said at Lake Tahoe Olympic training, he gave sick calls at 3 PM each day and gave whoever wanted anabolic steroids. It is not automatic that things will be okay for high-performance taking anabolic steroids. His severe quadricep pull in Hawaii came from too much strength, and his body could not tolerate this strength.

This probably happened with his back injury as well, in Germany in 1969, when he was too strong for his pants. I knew, many times over, that if I used my full strength, I was in danger of pulling a muscle or tendon. My current training was intended to get me used to high speeds every week. Tom showed me his shoulder on my visit and pointed to his collarbone. He hurt his shoulder at Tahoe, then shot it with cortisone many times, and his collarbone dissolved. He showed me the gap; he was playing the guitar. He had many talents. He bought a large church in SF from the money he made in Saudi Arabia and said he was in danger of losing it because of his legal bills defending himself from the Olympic committee.

"They have the Special Olympics, so why not 'Gay Olympics?' It is for what you and I want: sportsmanship, achievement, and inclusiveness."

He made money going to Saudi Arabia, and before he left, I objected to him going and helping a reactionary regime. In Budapest for the world indoor meet years later, I went out to dinner with Lee Evans, the coach of the US team, and John Smith (a world-class 400-meter runner) with the prince of Saud Arabia.

Seated around the dinner table sat officials, athletes, trainers, and health workers from all over Africa who were directly influenced by Tom. He founded many hospitals and brought in modern medicine and alternative medicine. I think I was a little rigid in condemning him for working for a reactionary regime. He did well; he was at Selma in the South for civil rights and marched for LGBT. A street was named after him in SF and a Waddell Health Center in SF.

Jack, Tom and I decided we needed to form a Bay Area track club that was run by athletes. We first called it the "Institute Track Club," but then the "Bay Area Striders." Except for Tom and I, we were all Black. Our club won the outdoor national title, and the next year, they stopped being team champions.

Several athletes, including hurdler Larry Livers from the club, called and said our coach was taking over and telling the athletes what to do.

I said, "Meet with him and then fire him, you are in charge."

I was told later that he objected, saying that he could not do that because coaches were in charge.

"No," they said to him, "we are in charge."

We never had a coach after that; who needs a coach? We were all pretty happy and coached each other.

Chapter 22: The UW Hall of Fame, My Disgust and Father Giving Permission to Get World Record, My UW Record Purged by the New Coach I Gave the Job to, Siddha Yoga and Old Friends, Material Needed to Get the World Record

In 1992, I was voted into the Hall of Fame of the University of Washington. At first, there was an on-field ceremony with other inductees; my father and I had VIP seats in the stadium. Below, on the field, we watched each honored inductee be announced into the UW Hall of Fame. My name came up as 80,000 fans cheered. The announcer boomed my name.

"Dr. Phil Shinnick, NCAA All-American, US Olympian, world record in the long jump, most points ever scored in track and field, Husky record in the high jump, captain of the US national team for Pan Conference Championships, and two medals in high jump and sprint relay, etc."

However, in the program, they mentioned that my world record was being discounted. This depressed and distracted me from this great moment. I could not shake my mood.

I stared at the floor and could not watch, and I did not really listen.

My father looked at my face and said, "Phil, they are honoring you below. Can't you hear this? You seem disinterested. What is wrong?"

"I am still unhappy about my world record at Modesto. It took them 30 years to induct me when Brian got in within five years. Now, women can pole vault what he did. I was told by a fraternity brother who was on the selection committee that I was left off because of my politics, and he had to argue hard to get me in."

I was glum, not so happy, even offended by the fuss.

He called the athletic director, Barbara Hedges, over and said, "Phil has represented the US all over the world. Would you help with his world record?"

She said, "Yes, write me a letter filling in the details, and I will support Phil."

Years before, the then-athletic director, Joe Kearney, whom I met while in graduate school and had a higher-up position in the UW administration, asked me if I knew of someone to be a track coach at the UW. I had been training at UCLA.

Ken Shannon was the assistant coach under Jim Bush. I saw Ken on the field when I trained at the old dirt track before the new track stadium was built; he coached the weight events. I saw him in the weight room, and we lifted together with Russ Hodge. I knew that the UW football players were not very strong. Even as a senior, I could outlift any football player; they just didn't know how to do it.

In football, weight conditioning was an afterthought. I told Kearney Ken that he would change the sports program and that Shannon could show them how to lift weights. John Dobroth, a friend of the 7' 2" high jumper, told me that Ken manipulated one of the shot putters psychologically, but I thought he would be good for Washington.

The first thing he did when he got the job was take away my long jump and high jump records. This was politically motivated; he was a born-again Christian. Later, his track athletes complained to me that the squad was split over their beliefs and that anabolic steroid use by weight events was under the table. I presume he learned this at UCLA when this was the norm. His weight men won national titles. I called Kearney and told him Shannon had taken away my records. I never mentioned drug use to him.

Kearney did not know what to do, so I told him I would prove it. I dug through the press clippings to get the results for the 1965 national championships in Balboa Stadium.

Otis Burrell, Ed Caruthers, and McClellan jumped 7', and I jumped 6' 11" for the second-highest height. I had taken a fall quarter off for the 1964 Olympic games, so at Balboa, I was still an undergraduate. Shannon maintained this after I graduated. The long jump record was more difficult.

At Modesto, Mike Thrall (UW hurdler), and Coach Stan Hiserman, were at the meet and pit, as well as others. Plus, I found clippings of the officials voting to accept my record. UW sprinter Steve Brown, a judge from Yakima, certified the letter. Kearney changed the records back. This took a year to prove and for only seconds of performance.

I found that doing daily Zazen Zen meditations and yoga without doctrinaire philosophy made it possible to have a decent, healthy life away from being upset with my world record and the injustices that I had gone through. So, in the 1990s, I attended regular retreats at a Siddha yoga retreat center in South Fallsburg, New York.

My seating assignment for the intensive (I was taking the third Blue Pearl advanced retreat as well as the general intensive) was next to Fr. Tom Toomey. Toomey (remember he gave me the plane ticket to build the church in Alaska) was now the chaplain at the ashram.

"What is this all about?" I asked him.

He told me that people needed a guru (Gurumaya was the guru after Muktananda died) when they could not find themselves (or Self).

Earlier, he met Muktananda in LA and joined the ashram there. He felt that he did not want to wear robes anymore. This cloistered community of men and women fit him well, and he then moved to South Fallsburg when Mukananda died.

He pointed to a man walking by, saying, "He was a saint."

I asked, "Why?"

And he said, "Because he had a bitch for a wife, and he stayed with her!"

So, he was still into chastity, some misogyny in him from his earlier life. When Muktananda left the ashram at South Fallsburg, he was in charge. When the guru left, all the top leadership and others started sharing beds. Tom was red hot over this, so he came to the city to be treated by me for anger. Anger of the liver causes heat to rise, drying out his eyes. He had glaucoma. He did not appreciate his own anger over this and needed to talk about it. Sort of old school.

Dana Hall, my UW girlfriend whom I unwisely separated from when she would not declare she believed in God (everywhere is God), was in line in the lunchroom. Fr. Toomey knew of her. I had not seen Toomey since my undergraduate days twenty years earlier.

In my last Blue Pearl session, after meditating on the third eye for days, a red spot appeared over my third eye. People said this was an auspicious sign. I thought that in India, they painted this as a superficial sign. To me, it is not a big deal; others may not be able to be one-pointed. I learned this in athletics.

Near the end of the Blue Pearl intensive, I descended into an abyss of open space; a sort of grey-white appeared, with silence and vibration, able to see off in all directions. Then, a face came before me and said,

"So? What are you going to do with your world record."

In a flash, the abyss and face dissolved.

Before, in 1992, my father gave me a dispensation to pursue the world record and expelled me from not doing it by thinking this was an ego trip and selfish but injustice, and I had a right not to be overcome by bad feelings. This appearance in my meditation gave me the go-ahead that this was also a spiritual issue.

This prompted me to call Primo Nebiolo, who was now president of the World Athletic Federation (IAAF). He told me they never received an application from the US, and first, it had to be approved by the US and then forwarded back to him. He said he understood that at the meet, only one wind gauge was on the field and that he did not record my jump. He referred me to Robert Hyman, the editor of the world record book.

Only track and field news had a contrary position, saying the flags on the field represented a .4 meters per second overage. Later, it was discovered that the flags were high up in the stadium, and lower flags on the field showed allowable wind.

Grant Birkinshaw, a New Zealand statistician, recruited an independent science group in New Zealand to test the video of my jump, which showed the flags on the field. They duplicated these conditions in a wind tunnel and reported their finding that the wind was well under the allowable.

At 13, Grant was in a movie theater and saw a news flash that I had broken the world record and showed my jump. This changed his life; he wanted to be a long jumper, become the national youth champion, and receive a scholarship to the UW for track.

In his freshman year, he jumped 25' 1", which is a new frosh record. Shannon also wanted him to do the triple jump, which he had not trained for. On one of his jumps, his knee gave out and tore it apart from the force, surgery, and permanent injury. He retained his scholarship, helped out with track, and entered the Graduate School of Public Affairs like me. He called me out of the blue as I was preparing the documentation and wanted to help. Grant prepared the brief presented to US Track and Field and gave the oral arguments to the record committee.

That was a big problem! Olan Cassell, the executive director of USA Track and Field, perhaps mad that it was I who was chosen for the top position at FISU in 1965 over him, never responded to the 1990s Hedges letter which my father initiated.

Cassell was from Texas and was chosen to lead US T&F after athletes (Connolly, Dobroth, Power, and others) rose up to object to the lack of leadership. We wanted an athlete at the helm. He was chosen because he was a conservative. I knew that he would never allow approval of my record. In fact, I had to wait 9 years for him to be gone.

In starting my search, Guy Benjamin, a Stanford, Miami Dolphins, and SF 49er quarterback, drove with me to interview Tom Moore, the meet director at Modesto. As a young athlete, Moore broke the world record in the high hurdles at a meet at Cal; there was no wind gauge. Brutus Hamilton, trusted coach at Cal, testified that when Tom ran the hurdles, the ashes on his cigarette did not fall off, and there was no wind.

This one testimony got him the WR. I asked Tom why, after the meet, officials voted to approve my record, but he did not submit it. He said that Olan Cassell told him if he submitted it, he would take away the sanction for the Modesto California Relays. That this was his whole life, the most important thing he had ever done. Apparently, he was ashamed of what he did but would try to change this. He wrote a strong letter indicating from his personal experience on the field next to the long jump and judgment it was fair.

Before the meet, he told Leon Glover, the wind official, not to record anyone in the long jump except Boston since they only had one gauge and the junior college and open competition needed recordings. He thought Boston would beat the record. Boston jumped after me, so he was right next to the runway and saw my jump. I think he was relieved, happy to see Guy and me, and was a fan of both of us. He was very old and died not many years later. He recorded my jumping for many years.

I drove over to the San Jose area to see Leon Glover. I had called him for years and sent him letters, but no answer. One day after dogging him, he picked up the phone, glad to hear from me, and we set a time to meet. He had a big conference room next to his Tyco Electronic office, stacks of paper piled three feet high on the floor, and his desk.

I asked him, "What is all this?"

He said, "Everyone wants me to do something or other, and I get a lot of mail every day. But I never open any of them and stack them neatly in piles, and I never listen to my phone messages. I mostly avoid everyone."

They all wanted him to do something.

"So, what do you do? Do you have a boss?"

"Probably, but not interested."

He was the senior guru. He liked to play the clarinet and collect hot rods, and he had a 34 Ford, an old Corvette, and a 59 Porsche Super Coupe.

"I make things out of the Earth, from the very beginning, and create things."

"Like what?"

"Anything, a toaster, things that interest me, they leave me alone."

He had thick glasses, had a Stanford chemistry Ph.D., and was a mad scientist but loved sports and officiating, proud to see world records like mine. We adjourned into the conference room just for him off his office, with wrap-around windows. He sat in the middle of a wooden conference table, and I was at the end. He started.

In the 30s, the Nazis tried to figure out what speed of wind would help an athlete, putting a large fan behind runners for a 100. They had eight runners who were instructed to run together at one speed, repeating with the variance of a wind turbine. At one joule or 2 MPS, they noticed some difference.

"So, they had to run many 100s back-to-back?" I said.

"Yes, so not that scientific, but this became the standard."

They ignored the actual wind conditions on the field and did not see how difficult it was to match a time for eight athletes together. Perhaps they got warmed up after repeating some 100s. They had hand timers.

He continued, "Tom Moore said just record Boston in the long jump. The gauge was in the space between the long jump runway and the finish of the races. I recorded a 220 hurdle race at the time you jumped. I always left the gauge on. I listened to the whirl of the blade and could tell within .1 meters per second what the velocity of the wind was. No turning on or off; if I heard it over, then I could record that, under, no recording, since it was legal. I remember all your jumps for the subsequent years. You never had an illegal jump.

"In the 1968 Olympic trials at Tahoe, you were the only athlete to have fair jumps. Boston, Beamon, and Mays had wind-aided jumps. As with other meets, you were sensitive to the vicissitudes of the wind and knew that when there was a lull, the wind was rarely constant. The wind at Modesto comes from the west, hits the stands, goes around, and then swirls. Peter Snell got a real blast for several seconds on one lap on the top turn in his mile run. He came within .1 from the world record."

175

Leon Glover wrote a supportive letter saying, in his professional opinion, that at Modesto, he was aware of the wind and confident that my jump was legal. It all took me years to fly out to California and do historical research. As I mentioned, Hedges wrote a fine letter to Olan Cassell, who did not answer. Then, he was ousted, had too many enemies, pissed off many people, and finally, he was voted out. Craig Masback took over. I called him, but he never answered.

I got more help than Grant. Lee Evans, an old buddy with Bay Area Striders, shared headlines for our victories in indoor and outdoor track, and we trained together at Tahoe. He broke the WR in Mexico in the 400 meters in under 44 seconds, the first ever to break 44. He won the gold just ahead of Larry James. We were old, old friends, and he had been in Africa coaching and came back to the US to get an SS retirement, then went back to Africa. Lee became an assistant coach at Washington. I told him about Masback not returning my letters or calls. He had a plan; he had been named head coach for the indoor world championships in Budapest, my old stomping grounds with FISU. He invited me to share a room and then got me credentials and food. He watched Masback's daily route.

In the morning or later, he went to the Nike hospitality room in an area in Budapest. We arrived there at 9 AM and waited. Then, around noon, he showed up, but I had to go take a pee. Not knowing when he would arrive, I held it as long as possible but had to go. Lee came running into the restroom and said Masback was there. When he tried to leave, my athletes cornered him and surrounded him. When he tried to break the circle, they chest-butted him. He saw me coming and again tried to break ranks; they held him.

Lee said, "Craig, you need to support Phil's application for the American record."

He looked around at all the Black faces but could not get away. He reneged and said, "Okay, see Bill Roe, the president, for the procedure."

I called Bill Roe, who had been a UW coach and now a Western University cross-country coach. Grant and I now had an avenue for an appeal, and Roe showed us how to submit it to the records committee. This came eleven years from the Hedges letter to Cassell. I got the hearing in 2003.

Chapter 23: Performance and Restorative Drugs in Sport, Injured Trying to Make the 1972 Olympic Team, Planning Peace Gathering in Munich and Upstaged by Black September PLO Youth Group and Israeli Athletes Killed, Injured Again

Athletes are now tested in training by the World Anti-Doping Agency, and if they are not home after notification, they are punished. For several years in the late '60s, drug use among my fellow Olympians and world-class athletes was unknown to me, even though I was on the field daily with athletes at UCLA.

Slowly, I heard about sophisticated practices of taking vitamins, anti-inflammatories, a wide variety of anabolic steroids, and what doses and when to take them. You had to be a pharmacologist.

Year by year, I learned more to keep up with new drugs and what was available; this was a second job. A hammer thrower, George Frenn, had a medical cart with syringes for B-12 shots, other vitamins, and things I try to forget for Tom Waddell, MD, who understood all of this from his medical training. It was not a big deal to him. For me, I needed another master's degree (in pharmacology) to know about performance-enhancing and restorative drugs.

Athletes get injured all the time. John Pennell, world record pole vaulter Olympic medalist, pulled a muscle before the 1968 Olympic trials. After 1964, he had a serious car accident, which took him over a year to recover. He came back and then pulled his hamstring (I saw it) but was back in top shape quickly. With an injury recovery, anabolic steroids can get you back to where you were much faster.

In Pennell's case, he just got back to where he was. So, it was restorative and not performance-enhancing. Without all his accidents and his hamstring pull, he probably could have gone higher.

To me, it seemed just another obstacle since it created a moral dilemma. Too complicated. I decided not on vitamins, anti-inflammatories (which hurt my stomach), or anabolic steroids. I did not need these steroids, just good food, rest, meditation, yoga, and mind training under the stress of competition.

To this day, some 50 years later, personally and now in my medical practice, with experience in non-surgery, non-drug orthopedics, physical medicine, and acupuncture, I find no need for drugs for rehabilitation or performance.

In preparation for the 1972 Olympic games in Eugene, Oregon, the US Olympic trials were nearing. Harold Connolly, Tom Waddell, Jack Scott, Gary Power, and myself conspired to have a morning of international peace at the 1972 Munich Olympics. My future was uncertain; I had to make the team. I would try to be there. We made up buttons with peace signs, posters, leaflets to be distributed, and a program. It was set for 10 AM and was to be held in the Olympic Village for athletes only. A whole suitcase was stuffed full for our event. I learned from my FISU experience how internationalism can change the mood of athletes.

Carol and I were broke and living off of my military stipend to go back to school at Cal, and her baton was twirling. Each summer since college, she went to a twirling camp in California for high school baton twirlers, which left me with taking care of Shannon and Quincey for long periods of time, the merry pranksters in Berkeley planned at night mischief Dave and I had kids and family, others were footloose and fancy-free, able to attack the corrupt system.

To me, they were anarchists and seemed happiest plotting disruption; some were even making small bombs, yet I had never heard of any going off. The conversation drifted into my ears, whispering about targeting war facilities when no people were around. I was out of these conversations. I focused on racism, sexism, drug use, and my own Olympic revenge.

Plotting my redemption from the disaster of Modesto and what I felt was my dishonor and discrediting. I felt this was an ego thing. Why was I so set on my honor, trying to win the Olympics? It was a deep pain and got worse as I got older, nightly dreams for 30 years, circling the Olympic stadium, trying to find the door into the field to compete. Long paths, labyrinths, many people, conversations, trying to get clues to find the right door.

My training not only put me to where I was at 20, uninjured, my old injuries healed after a year of no competition. I was fast and strong and could run hard uphill and not get tired. I was the most flexible I had ever been, doing yoga twice a day, even on my rest day off every fourth day. My speed was consistently fast and easy. Charlie Green was a super Olympic sprinter with whom we roomed in the officers' club in Ireland. He taught me what to do. He said, "Do not push off; it is a quick action with the thighs on the upswing, quite different. He ran 9.4 in high school."

Following his advice, I now had quickness, which required no strain. I made the Olympic long jump mark at Modesto a month earlier at 26' 5 ½" and advanced to the final US Olympic trials. I decided to just take a jump or two in Seattle for the US national championships. I debated for weeks whether to skip this since it meant nothing, but then I got a free ticket to Seattle.

I stayed with Carol's family in Mercer Island. I was 29. Carol's father, Virgil, never understood going for a Ph.D. at Cal. Why didn't I just get a job like the one offered to me, to be associate director of the Graduate School of Public Affairs at Washington two years earlier or to work for the police chief?

I took the policeman's exam and scored 100 in the physical and written exams during my "Mayor of Seattle" intern period. I took many civil service tests to evaluate for reliability and validity. Virgil wondered why, at 29, I was still competing. Because at that time, athletes quit at 24.

One Thanksgiving in graduate school at the UW, on a cold, drizzling day before dinner, he went with me to a dirt track. I did three 330 runs pretty fast. After the second one, I threw up, and he saw this.

He always asked me, "Why don't you just quit? Why do you suffer so much? You are not competing."

I knew I would be in a world-class competition in a year or so, and I was preparing myself. This same refrain became more intense; to his benefit, I do not think anyone besides Carol understood an athlete's heart. She was a good match for me. Like me, she used the summers to train every day even though her season was months away. That is where she and I came together, at the Husky Stadium. Virgil's thinking was common for nonathletes.

Every day in 1966, I thought about what I needed to do to maintain top shape, even though my energy went into my graduate work, my job at the mayor's office, and caring for my newborn Shannon.

On the day of the nationals, I went to the UW stadium, intent on getting an easy jump and leaving. Walking onto the field from the underground tunnel, I got a whiff of the artificial track and infield. It clogged my nostrils; it was not the sweet smell of the grass infield and black cinder track. It was all plastic, and it gave off a bad smell. I had limited intention; a national championship did not interest me. I saw Jacques Pani from France and others I did not pay much attention to. Beamon and Boston were gone.

My steps were on; I brought my left foot jumping shoe, an Adidas, which was firmly built, with a built-up toe and solid plastic sole. It would not break like the one at Modesto, which did not have a built-up insole at the front to catapult up and out. For my right non-jumping foot shoe was a Puma, which is a super-fast sprint shoe. I took just one pair; I would take two jumps and go home.

On my last run-through, which was lightning fast, my Puma flew off my foot completely in shatters, similar to my third take-off at Modesto. I withdrew from the competition since after my father-in-law scolded me, I rushed out of the house (to avoid him) to get to the stadium and did not take my complete competitive bag. Virgil did not go.

They had no shoes in stock at the stadium, and my in-law had to rush my other shoe to the stadium, which would take half an hour. I asked the officials to delay the competition for half an hour. They would not! They were not kind to me, as Bill Bowerman was delaying competition for the rain in the 1964 college nationals. I climbed up the stadium stairs to sit with my mother. She questioned why I was dropping out. She knew I would do well. She was at Modesto earlier for my qualifying jump of 26' 5 ½".

She said, "Phil, just borrow some shoes from other competitors."

She said this several times. I did not say anything, and then I relented. Norman Tate was in the competition, and we were on the national team indoors in the Soviet Union in 1969. We were the same size, and I liked Tate.

Should I borrow just the right shoe or use his jumping shoe as well? I went back and forth and then decided to use his complete set. I noticed even years before he used longer spikes than me. Should I try the left jumping shoe? It would give me more lift off the board. I went with both of his shoes; my run-through was fast, and I felt good. I did not have shorter spikes or a wrench to change his spikes.

When my turn came, I hit the board perfectly and felt a tremendous lift, like at Modesto in 1963, which was my best jump in 9 years. The end of the pit looked near; I was fine through the first rotation of my double hitch kick, then my left lateral hamstring went into a spasm and pulled, and I aborted the jump. I pulled and injured my hamstring; I could not stop the rotation because of my speed.

As my leg continued in rotation, I felt a sharp pain. This was eighteen days before the final 1972 Olympic trials. Remorse overwhelmed me, the past two years gone, injury-free training, and the best shape of my life.

I flew to Berkeley, saw a doctor who injected it with an anti-inflammatory and sent me to rehab, which I did every day. This was very painful. She kept taking the hamstring further and further in range of motion. I was then able to sprint near full speed days before my event. I flew to Eugene and stayed in a dorm room.

The night before the trials, I heard a knock on the door, and Mike Speno, a distance runner whom Jack had been coaching, brought his new wife, Dervaca, 20 years his senior, who implored me to have her work on me. Mike left the room and left me with her. She treated me like she was tenderizing meat, very aggressively, getting into my hamstring with her thumbs, which was very painful. I was in shock! That night, all night, my hamstring quivered and went into spasms.

Afterward, for ten years, I had a hole in my hamstring at the injury site; the PT and Dervaca had ripped the fibers to get it to release. I competed in Eugene with caution. I hit the board and jumped near 25'.

On my next jump, I had good speed, near top speed, and feared my hamstring would not take the force of a world-class jump. When I hit the board, I let go, blocked my jump, and ran through the pit, withdrawing from the competition.

I did not think my hamstring could withstand jumping in the finals the next day or a jump necessary to make the finals. A week later, I asked Ben Vaughn, national sprint champ and near the world record in 100 and 200 meters, to enter a 100 race with me in an all-comers meet at my favorite track in Contra Costa. I promised him that I would not beat him and that if I went ahead at 90 meters, I would let up.

My start was fast, and I was way ahead of Vaughn. I felt like hell on wheels. At 90, I was ahead, I let up, and he surged ahead and ran 9.4. We were both happy. I needed just one more week before the 1972 US trials, which I did not have. This ended my career. I needed a job.

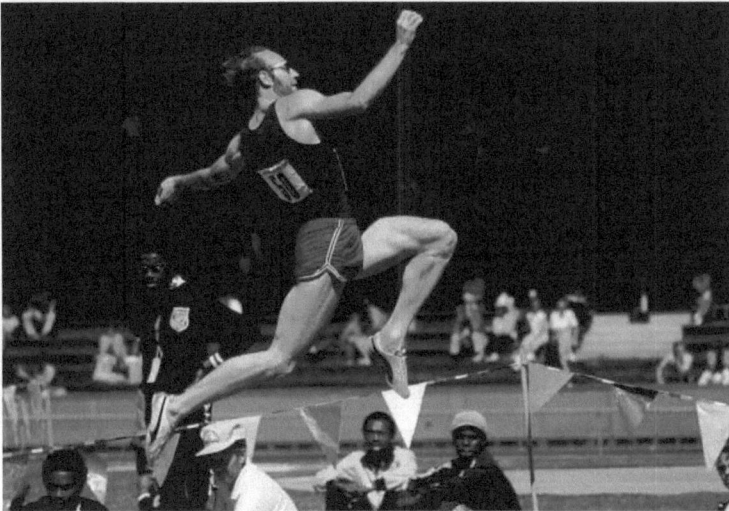

1972 Phil Shinnick Final Olympic Trials in Eugene, Oregon.
Competing with a pulled hamstring 18 days earlier.

At the 1972 Munich Olympics, the day of our big international peace event in the Olympic Village (I was home), Gary Power (a hurdler and friend) had managed to smuggle in all the buttons, leaflets, and posters of the event for 10 AM September 4th, 1972.

Early that morning was Black September (4th of September). A youth group of armed Palestinians attacked the Israeli dorm, taking hostages known as the "Munich Massacre." .

West German police ambushed the two helicopters at Furstenfeldbruck air base with nine hostages on board. The athletes were all murdered; the police were ill-prepared. Hours before in the village, two Israeli athletes fought back, Moshe Weinberg and Hossie Romano, and were killed!

Chapter 24: The Politics of Getting the American Record, World Athletics Politics, and Teasing Seb Coe, New President at the Helm

Ralph Boston lived in Peach Tree City, and when I called him, he agreed to help me get the record. Years earlier, when I called him, he had just sold his interest in a radio station and bought a cleaning service for offices. He was having all sorts of problems with employees and accounts. His uncle, when he complained, said, "If you buy the dog, you get the fleas." This seemed to appease his anxieties.

Boston, Lee Evans, and Grant Birkinshaw from New Zealand came to the Records Committee for our presentation. Bill Roe, the President of US Track and Field, gave us this opportunity. He was a former coach at Washington, then became a cross-country coach at Western Washington University.

Grant made the presentation; we noticed a face in the room who was not a member of the Records Committee. We objected. Bob Hersh, an Olan Cassell shadow, insisted to the Records Committee that it was okay. This intruder wrote for the publication *Track and Field News*, which printed an editorial rejecting my record. Bob Hersh was an editor for Track and Field News and brought in this spy—a plant.

The Records Committee was receptive. Athletes could now be on this committee. Several young Black faces were there, and I could see they were respectful to Boston and Evans, two Olympic Champions and World Record holders. The Record Committee voted to accept my record. I found out later that Hersh overruled them. He said they had no authority.

Grant had all the testimonies of officials that Hyman required to actualize the 1939 rule. Hyman was quoted adding newspaper accounts, particularly the Sacramento Bee. The writer was a sailor and knew zephyrs. "Not a whisper," he wrote. This supplemented the UW Athletic Director Hedges' letter, which was sent almost ten years ago.

The head of the Records Committee, an older man, sat me down in an old desk chair next to him and huddled close after the Record Committee decision. He had his hand on my arm and said, "The Records Committee has turned your record down. We claimed there was no wind, and Hersh, in the meeting, insisted that clear evidence showed the wind was about 1 MPS (well under the allowable); therefore, your record was rejected." An oxymoron.

I said to him, "If you release this to the press, they will think you are a fool. You should be careful with this mischief."

He came even closer and said, "I am very sorry about this. The Executive Committee has final authority, and you should go to them right now."

He kept his hand on my forearm and added, "I am so sorry about this."

I think he knew their mischief would not hold.

John Caplin (motormouth, they called him since he could lay down a rap as good as any Black rapper), head coach of the 2000 US Olympic team and a 220, 440 speedster from many years coach at Washington State University, was now Executive Director of the Executive Committee. He was standing next to the long jump pit in 1963 when I jumped; he knew the real story.

The day before, Grant, Lee, John, and I went to the hotel bar. When we entered, we saw a sea of Black faces all together. This is difficult to describe. I knew them all, trained with them, or competed in the same meet. When they saw us, a semi-circle opened up and engulfed us into a circle. We huddled closer, and all eyes were on John Chaplin.

"Do you support Phil?" they asked.

"Yes. I have always supported Phil. I was standing near the long jump pit, saw the jump, and knew it was legal," John replied.

Something happened. A solidarity came over all of us. With John's comments, we were now in charge and, at last, had power. Words started coming out from deep down, one by one.

John said, "I had a very difficult life, then I thought of Phil. If you can overcome injustices, then this gave me strength."

This continued, and all the troubles, racism, and suffering of each athlete poured out. Everyone was in tears. We went into a separate world, and all our barriers were down; we were one. Life is tough and painful, but you must persevere and stand together as brothers.

I entered the Executive Committee room, and everyone looked up. *Shinnick is here,* I thought, recognizing officials from Oregon, California, and Washington—most were at Modesto and had seen the jump. John turned to me and said, "It is done. You are approved. You have the American Record."

That was it, done, an American Record. I waited around outside. Then, I saw Hersh go into the room and come out, then in again and out again. There was a lot of noise. I then left.

Caplin later told me, "Hersh came into the Executive Committee room and told them they could not approve my record. We said, 'We just did. You have no right to be in this room.'"

Hersh was mad. He came back several times with the same response. Then, Hersh became red-faced and heated and started yelling, "You cannot do this."

Chaplin then said to Hersh, "Bob, if you do not get your sorry ass out of this room, I will headbutt you and drag you out by your heels. You are recused from any dealings with Shinnick at the international level because of your political and personal bias toward Phil."

As it turned out, Hersh never recused himself internationally.

Chaplin meant it; he would have headbutted Bob Hersh. John is a tough guy, very popular with athletes, and not afraid of anything. I saw him run the quarter mile in college, fast at the beginning and fast at the end, fearless, brilliant in the 220 also, and built like a linebacker. Very strong.

Lee had an idea to get IAAF approval. He was named US Coach for the World Indoor Championships in Budapest. He would get me credentials, share a room, and introduce me to the new President, Lamine Diack, and the secretary of the IAAF. Lamine Diack was a 25, long jumper from Senegal. I thought because of this and my time competing and coaching in Dakar, Senegal, we would have some common ground. We could not get an appointment with Elder Diack. The word was out that if you wanted to get to Diack, you had to go through Papa—Diack's son. When I saw Papa, he had bodyguards in full African robes, marching around with a regal demeanor. I thought there was no getting near him or having a conversation. We had nothing to offer him; he was not an athlete.

Lee and I devised a second approach. Lee figured out that Diack came into his office very early—at 7 AM. We would go see him early since we could not get an appointment. We arrived at 6:30 AM and waited. At 7 AM, he entered his secretary's office, where we were seated. Lee knew him and said, "We have some business with you."

He demurred and ignored us. Lee saw the open door to his conference room, and we jumped in. We sort of pulled him into the room because of our brashness and his respect for Lee, who had coached in Africa. Lee sat on the middle side of the conference table, and I took a chair and sat right next to Diack. He grunted. He looked like a dog with his neck and hair up, sort of bent over, elbows on the table, and facing forward.

Lee said to Diack, "We came to get your approval of the American Record and approve it as a World Record."

He pulled out a piece of paper, pointed to it, and said, "All that we want is the right number on the WR application, and we will approve it."

"Just a number on paper is all you want? A computer or robot can do this. What is the use of people involved?" I said.

"Yes. That is it. We only want the right number," he said.

Diack did not like Lee and me asking for his support; his anger was evident. Lee and I looked at each other and thought there was no use in staying, so we left.

Lee then introduced me to the Hungarian secretary of the IAAF. Each time we tried to approach him, he seemed to scurry away. I think he knew we were looking for support for my record, and he wanted to avoid us.

One time, we were after him and could not find him. We saw his shoes sticking out from under a curtain and knew he was hiding from us. We waited around the area where he worked and finally found him. Lee quickly told my story.

In response, he repeated what Diack said, "Only the right number is needed, that is all."

He quickly changed the subject, saying how proud he was that his son was the announcer for the meet. He also was a meet announcer, and how lucky he was to have landed this job. I was resentful that a person like Hersh went into power through announcing, a big mouth, not an athlete.

Lee made himself invisible after that, so he stood behind those curtains (his shoes not showing) and evidently overheard a conversation about my WR situation; officials were buzzing on this topic. Lee heard two issues about my situation: first, if they approved my record based on injustice, they would have to deal with many cases of injustice. The next was a financial concern. WRs were given a million dollars since professional athletes could compete, but they did not want to give money.

Our trip to Budapest did not go well; their minds were made up. A Chinese official, Lou Depeng, was on the IAAF Council. Perhaps he would help me since I had been in China and worked with the Sports Committee on the history of the exclusion of China from the Olympics. Xiao, my babysitter for my one-year-old son Kent, at 6 AM at the Columbia pool while I swam with the triathlete swim team. He was Chinese from Shanghai. He tutored Kent for 20 years in Chinese and mathematics. I sent Xiao to China on a mission to find Lou DePeng. He went to the Beijing Sports Headquarters and tracked him down at his home. Lou suggested that I meet in Birmingham, England, for the European Indoor Championships.

Traveling to Birmingham and going to the indoor arena, I sat down in an empty seat and looked at the program. Lynn Davies, the long jump 1964 Olympic Champion, now UK President of track-and-field, had a full page in the program. I called the usher over and asked, "Where is Davies?"

He motioned just five rows up where he was sitting.

Davies was in the first row of the top tier. I just climbed a few stairs up, stood under him, and said, "Hi."

He knew me. I told him my story with Diack. He came down out of his seat and put his arm around me for Diack to see. Lamine Diack was milling around near us; as Diack approached, Lynn shut him out to make him suspicious. Diack walked by, eyeing us.

"Let's go to the UK sports VIP room," Lynn said.

We ascended further up in the arena. Security said to me, "You do not have the proper credentials."

Davies told the security, "He is an honored guest of mine."

There were food perks, a view of all the meet below with a glass panoramic vision, and all the UK sports officials. I was so grateful for his help that I tried to take off my Olympic undersuit long-sleeve warm-up. He waved me aside, "No need for this."

I would have given him anything I had. He recognized my generosity. He had a plan, which he shared. Seb would come to the room shortly, and Lynn said to ignore him.

Seb would look across the room to scope things out, see me talking to someone he would not recognize, and want to know who that was and why we were huddled. Seb, like a fish looking at a fly, circled around. Lynn then made sure Seb could not see who I was, turning away each time. Finally, Lynn opened up, turned to Seb, and said, "Do you know Phil Shinnick?"

Then, Seb circled around, and we rotated as well. "Yes, we have gone a few rounds," Seb said.

Seb visited Oregon during his competitive days and was friends with Steve Prefontaine, a star distance runner. I think he was exposed to our progressive athletic movement, which flourished during that era. Pre died in Eugene after a great race. He had been smoking a little weed at a house party with some beers, then drove his little sports car down the winding road of a steep hill, hit a curb, flipped over, and the car rested on him. He suffocated; no one was around to save him. Pre was a man who could go long periods at top speed with little oxygen, and then he died from lack of oxygen.

So, for a year, each month, I called Seb and said, "If you didn't support my WR, I would call upon the ghost of Prefontaine to haunt you."

Seb talked about going a few rounds. All three of us enjoyed the banter.

Seb Coe knew about my mission from Donna de Varona, a gold-medal Olympic swimmer who mentored young Seb Coe in his speeches. Donna came each day to UCLA, where all of us Olympians were training. I had met her on the 1964 Olympic team. She ran across Seb during her international travels for the Special Olympics and was a special guest of the International Olympic Committee. She knew IAAF Council members and approached them one by one for support of my WR, and each said the same thing. Each reported to her that Bob Hersh (whom John Caplin recused) visited each and implored them not to support my record. He was aggressive and arrogant.

In Birmingham, after my visit with Lynn Davies, I finally met Depeng. I brought him a small wooden box I purchased in Costa Rica for his family. Depeng gave me a medallion for the upcoming Beijing Olympics. We talked for an hour. I gave him the whole story about Olan, Hersh, etc. I talked about my sports trip to China in 1976 and my writings, with the help of the Chinese Sports Committee, on the exclusion of China from the Olympics. I told him about my help in getting China into the Olympics.

At the end, Depeng said, "Sounds like to me, this is the post-McCarthy fallout. You need to continue getting support from Council members."

Earlier, the IAAF rejection for my WR came in April of 2003, but in September, they sent me the disapproval letter. Alex Hartnet, a New York lawyer, Princeton soccer star, and entertainment lawyer, appealed to the Court of Arbitration for Sport (CAS), which turned the request down, saying it was time-bound. He found out that within 90 days after a decision by the IAAF, the CAS had to be notified.

I asked a New York City CAS lawyer, "How can I petition the CAS if I have not heard from them?"

He said, "You have to petition anyway, even though you have not been notified."

This seemed a bit crazy because the IAAF made sure I could not appeal.

All my avenues for an appeal to the IAAF rejection seemed closed. Things seemed dead, so I conjured up a way to get Seb Coe's attention, now Lord eddi, head of the London Olympics and President of the IAAF. In the early '60s, the IAAF was a mom-and-pop organization and put on no meets, but it evolved into many meets and a World Championship. Thus, they had lots of money from the meets and sponsors with a large bureaucracy from all over the world, and Seb was at the helm.

I sent him three interchanges about Steve Prefontaine's ghost, which I made up as sort of a joke. Grant Birkinshaw sent a video of my jump to a scientific organization to replicate within a wind tunnel the force necessary for the flag to flutter at the angle shown. Grant sent the conclusions and also prepared an updated brief to Lord Coe, saying that he should reconsider my jump for ratification. Seb created a second review process.

Chapter 25: Bob Hersh and Olan Cassell Tried to Stop US and World Record Meeting 1968 Olympic Teammates

Bob Hersh was not going away. All my trips to meet with Council members of the IAAF seemed fruitless; Hersh had treaded the territory. Olan Cassell, the Executive Director of US T&F, did not respond to the 1994 UW request to consider my WR for ten years. Remember Tom Moore, the Meet Director at Modesto, where I broke the record? He told me that Cassell would not sanction Moore's meet if he supported my record.

Cassell and Hersh were ousted in a vote and created a new show in town, which was very encouraging for me. I then prepared a detailed summary of my case for the new council representative of US T&F, and I sent it to her. Months went by, but I got no answer. I shortened my synopsis to her to make things easier. I contacted the new president, and his response to me was all about the money he had raised. Things went dead at US T&F; they were all chasing money and building careers.

After my letter to the new president, he asked the new council representative for advice. She answered, "I am not going to take a stand one way or the other."

In other words, she represented the US on the IAAF Council, but she was not going to support the US 2003 decision of an American Record. I wondered if reading the brief was too much for her.

During my competing years, Modesto was just one of many outdoor meets around the US, with big crowds and world-class foreign athletes coming to these meets to challenge the best. At one time, US T&F's office was in New York. I visited it years ago and saw only a few rooms, which mostly store national uniforms. A part-time, retired military person and a secretary were the complete offices.

Cassell moved the headquarters to Illinois, in the heartland, away from the National Indoor Championships in Madison Square Garden. When I came East in 1972 after getting through my oral and written exams for a Ph.D., I accepted a faculty position to teach at Rutgers. I was thinking of jumping indoors. The Garden was refurbished, and there was no room for the jumping events; thus, it could not hold the Nationals. I took this personally since my sports career seemed finished.

Years went by, perhaps ten years during Hersh's crusade to thwart me, then the new do-nothing Hersh appointee, the IAAF councilwoman for the US, which meant I had to outwait her tenure, another number of years.

The year 2018 was the 50th anniversary of the 1968 Olympic team (remember, in 2003, my jump became an American Record) and a new election for the IAAF Council seat to renew this do-nothing woman or elect someone else.

I decided to go to the national conference. I called the woman in charge of the reunion and explained to her, "Although I did not compete in Mexico City, I was a member of the 1968 Olympic team by my participation at Flagstaff, Arizona, in a pre-Olympic meet against the German Olympic team."

She said, "I would check and get back to you."

Well, I was not on the list, so I could not come. I went anyway. My buddy, Tracy Sundlun, had been a manager of the Olympic team and now was on the executive committee like John Chaplin.

John Chaplin, a Washington native who ran the 200 and 400 and became the Washington State Coach, had also been next to the long jump pit at Modesto when I jumped. Sitting in the lobby by myself, Tracy showed up with Chaplin. I explained how this woman took no action on my record. He said, "She's made many people angry, and it's judgment day. I'm her supporter, and I'll talk with her."

That woman was up for election in several days. As Chaplin left, Tracy said to me, "Hersh is her mentor. He's supporting Willie Banks for a new council member of the IAAF." Willie Banks was a world-class triple jumper, had trained with me at UCLA, and was friendly toward me.

I was not welcome at the huge dinner for the team since I was not on the list. I decided to have dinner or a beer by myself in the hotel garden. Dick Fosbury called me and said, "The dinner needs you. You should be there, at least, for me. You are my guest."

I hurried over to the room, which was hard to find, but he found me wandering around the halls.

Each member of the 1968 Olympic team got up and gave a little speech. Foz seemed to be the last to talk. He got up and said to everyone that he had a confession, that he was coming out, and that he brought his partner as a guest—Phil Shinnick. The place went wild with glee, laughing, and hooting.

I stood up, put my hands together, and raised my arms to more shouts. I pointed to Ralph Boston, who was resting on his elbows tables away and said, "At Modesto in 1963, I jumped 27' 4" and beat Ralph and set a new World Record. Look at Ralph now; he is sitting straight up. He never liked it and still doesn't."

Ralph was at attention. I turned to Ed Cruthers, sitting at my table, and said, "In 1965 at Balboa Stadium at the Nationals, I gave you a real scare when I cleared 6' 11" and got the second-highest height."

I turned to Fosbury and said, "You are the 1968 Olympic Champion at 7' 4", but in 1965, against your team, Oregon State, I beat you in a hailstorm while jumping into sawdust on a hard take-off surface. You had this crazy form, almost breaking your neck in that pit, landing on the back of your neck. Porta pits saved you from being crippled."

I searched the room, but Bob Hayes was not there; he had died. "My single best performance was after the rainstorm in Tokyo when I could not get a good jump. We went to Osaka but could not jump because Boston and Hopkins (by ¾") placed above me in the US trials and only two per event."

I saw many shaking their heads, remembering that meet. I looked at Norm Tate, whose shoes I borrowed before my injury in Seattle. He raised his fist and hooted. I continued, "I got to run the high hurdles, but Rex Cawley decided not to run the 400 and wanted to run the highs. Bob Hayes did not show up for the meet, so I got to run the first leg of the 4x400 relay."

I looked at Mel Pender, who had been on the 1968 team, sitting across from me. "My feet never touched the ground on the first leg; I flew like riding a horse. After our winning race with Ashworth, Stebbins, and Carr running the next legs, Walter, an Olympic coach, came over and showed me his stopwatch and said I ran 10.1 around a turn, the fastest ever. My knees hurt for two months. This was the single best performance and privilege of my life."

I turned to the table to my left, where Bob Beamon, Olympic Champ who broke the World Record in 1968 in Mexico City, was sitting, and said, "Bob, I am not ignoring you; you did not talk to me much when we competed, but you eyed my steps and lined up on them before you jumped."

I walked over to his table, and he jumped up and hugged me with great affection. He said, "I missed you."

The room became very happy with loud claps; we were all united. Things had shifted.

The banquet was the next night. Tracy and I had planned to sit together, but as I was talking to him inside the banquet area near the door, reminding him of our agreement to sit together, an important official took his arm and said, "We have a place for you; the table is full, but you can come."

Tracy looked at me. I said, "Go."

Before he left, five of us were huddled, the leadership of US T&F. Out of the corner of my eyes, I saw happy Hersh walking to join in. I turned aside, not to be seen. He broke the circle, gleeful. He was to be inducted into the US T&F Hall of Fame that night. I understood then his drive for this honor as his crowning achievement.

Tracy turned to him and asked, "You know Phil Shinnick?"

He scooted away in half a run, like a scared rabbit. I had nowhere to go for a seat, so I looked at the exit to leave. Patty Van Wolvelaere (star hurdler on two Olympic teams) took my hand and said, "Come with me."

We sat next to Jim Ryan (my roommate in 1964 in San Dimas before the 1964 Games) with Martha Watson and some of my old friends. When they announced that all members of the 1968 Olympic team would stand up, she took my hand, and we stood up together. After we were seated, I turned to Jim to my left and said, "We share one thing, and that is the recognition of the Spirit."

"What did you say?" he asked.

"We both believe in the Spirit."

He seemed perplexed, then realized I meant the Father, the Son, and the Holy Spirit. His wife seemed to understand. Politically, we were miles apart, but we had done a peace initiative in Lawrence, Kansas when I was able to bring the Soviet National team to Kansas for the Kansas Relays.

At the 1970 Nationals in Miami, I was standing on the last turn when Ryan was battling Marty Liquori to the finish; he stopped just a few feet away from me. He quit the race. At the Kansas

Relays, I said that I understood why he stopped; his heart was no longer in the race. I understood this; I had taken two years off myself. He took time off and then came back in 1972 to get an Olympic Silver medal in Munich. His wife heard my comment. She said, "Jim stopping that day was the worst thing he ever did in his career; praise the Lord."

Jim made the Olympic team in high school. In the 1964 qualifying race, 30-year-old Jim Grelle was the best US miler. In the last few yards, he was angry, and he did not win, so he eased up to get third behind Tom O'Hara and Dyrol Burleson. Big mistake. Jim nipped him by inches and got third; he was off the team. His experience might have gotten him a medal after Burleson was boxed in; O'Hara was hurt, and Ryan did not qualify.

At the 2018 national conference, Willie Banks beat Hersh's shadow woman in the vote for the IAAF Council. I thought, *Now I have a chance.* It has been 16 years since Diack let Russian athletes who tested positive for drugs into the games for money. Later, in 2020, he was found guilty by trial and sentenced to two years in jail and fined well under what money his son and he stole.

Chapter 26: A Professorship at Rutgers, Muhammad Ali Comes Knocking, Joe Frazier, Arthur Ashe, the US Open and Apartheid, Maud Russel and Exclusion of China from the Olympics, Federal Subpoenas, Carter's Moscow Olympics Boycott, Escorting Soviet Athletes in the US

As an assistant professor of sociology and history at Rutgers University, I had agreed three years before to be the Athletic Director at Livingston College, one of the sister colleges of the Rutgers system.

One morning, I was hiding in my gym storage room to think through the big day ahead. I needed this quietness, conjuring up ways to deal with complex racial and athletic situations upcoming. But first, I needed to finish my Ph.D. dissertation, set up a Sports Studies program, and establish a Physical Culture and Sports Department. Time Magazine called Livingston College—the Harvard of public universities—by recruiting top scholars, paying them high wages, and admitting poor Whites, ghetto Blacks, and Puerto Rican immigrants. Community leaders recommended largely uneducated young leaders who showed promise. These students were given many years to get it together, retaining these students who flunked classes until they caught up. They were required to upgrade their writing and cognition skills since they had not had that opportunity. This took them longer than other students, but in the end, they got educated. It worked, but we had a dynamic, heated situation.

I heard a knock on the storage door; no one was in the office except me. Muhammad Ali, in a blue suit and briefcase, looked good and walked in. "Are you Phil Shinnick?"

I nodded my head.

"I heard about you. You are a World Record holder."

I was in top shape, lifting weights, running 10 miles every other day, doing yoga, playing basketball, being able to pin the ball on the backboard while defending a layup, and running (playing basketball) with the local professional basketball players on the weekend.

"I also heard you were a friend of Joe Frazier. I need to hear about that," Ali said.

"You must have gotten up in the middle of the night to get here at this time," I retorted.

"Yes, I got up at 4 AM to drive up here."

He opened his briefcase, which was full of scraps of paper, and pulled out a tape measure. "I need to measure you, then you can measure me."

He wrote down the figures: biceps, thighs, chest, calves, waist, height, weight (a scale in the back) 6' 4" and 180 pounds. Except for his deltoids, which were a little bigger but not much, we were the same. Boxers get measured before a fight, so he knew the routine and wanted to see how he and I measured up.

"Okay, how do you know Joe Frazier? Tell me all, every detail; I got time."

Satisfied, we measured up pretty well together.

One of the days on the 1964 US Olympic team in Tokyo, all Olympians who wanted to attend a gathering to meet some dignitaries could come and also have access to an art gallery. Stepping up onto the bus and going down the aisle, all seats seemed to be taken. I then saw an empty seat next to a Black athlete.

I asked him, "Can I sit next to you?"

He motioned for me to sit down. He reached out with his left hand to shake; his right hand was in a cast. He introduced himself to me, saying, "I'm Joe Frazier."

I said, "Phil Shinnick."

He said, "I heard about you."

I retorted by saying, "You got the gold medal."

"Yes," he replied.

"So, what about your hand?"

"I broke it in the early rounds. I worked around it, but it was painful. Later, I had it x-rayed and saw the break," he said.

"Where are you from?" I asked.

"Philadelphia and you?"

"Spokane," I replied.

We chatted for some time. After we were introduced to the dignitaries, we drifted to the art gallery as part of the Embassy. Upon reaching each painting, we took a moment to admire it before exchanging our thoughts. I think in the end, he liked landscapes, and I was an impressionist. I liked brazen colors. He liked the subtleties of the blue and gold of the sun, sky, and clouds, the green of flora, and flowers of scenes. He pointed these out to me. I talked about my hitchhiking through Europe and going to art galleries throughout Europe. He talked about the hood of his upbringing. This went on for several hours; we never got bored and went from room to room.

Back on the bus, he discussed each of his rounds, the opponent, and his strategy. I gave him my sad news about the weather and humiliation; rarely had I brought this up; no one wants to hear a sad story. He did not seem to mind; he knew life was tough, and he had seen his share of injustice. When we saw each other across the Olympic Village, we waved, but we never felt a need to pal around; already, we had a connection.

Ali talked, and I listened. I talked, and he listened; both of us relaxed. I think he needed an athlete at my level to open up to. So, he talked about White-directed racism, on and on, lots of rap on this. I shifted to Africa, slavery, and how the Black Northern Africans put Irish sailors who wandered into the Mediterranean into servitude. I told him about a dream I had where the feuding Blacks captured Royster (a Cal track captain and Livingston sports club director) and me. They skinned us alive. Still alive, I heard them say, "Which one is Royster, and which one is Shinnick?"

They could not tell us apart with the skin off. If racism is only skin deep, then this is superficial; perhaps racism is also economic and cultural. He talked about color as a flashpoint for hatred, so we went around and around, which we really enjoyed.

This took many hours. He then opened his briefcase and took out a small piece of paper from many. It was a poem; he had over a hundred of them. He asked me to read each and then comment. One by one, this went on for hours more. It appeared he needed to hear what I thought of each and then all of them as a summary. I knew, and he knew the answer—everything comes from the heart. He needed to hear this from me and was well pleased. I told him, "You should go up to the dorms and meet the captain of the football team, organizers, and leaders of the Black movement on campus."

I gave him the dorm and room number. Later, these athletes came to me, wide-eyed, and said, "Ali sat with us the whole afternoon and listened to us, never seeming tired of meeting more student-athletes. He was at home here; he was like one of us."

That night, he gave a speech right on because he understood the issues of the Black students. He gave a balanced racial talk that did not have hatred toward Whites. He gave an overview: Keep up your studies, learn to express yourself through writing and language and learn from each other and from other students. He packed the gym that night—3,000 came. He talked as one of them, talking about himself and his struggles to not kill Asians, his jail time, and who he was now.

In the early 1980s, it was a rainy day outside the US Open in Flushing Meadows. Arthur Ashe was there with a megaphone, leading chants against apartheid, and a small crowd gathered. I walked up to Ashe. Like Ali, Ashe knew about me, so he immediately turned to me and said, "Those White tennis players from South Africa are my friends. I have more in common with them than Black athletes in the US; it breaks my heart to protest against those who are playing now. They feel like brothers to me."

He was very upset. He wanted to fight against apartheid, but he thought boycotting the US Open seemed the right political move. Yet, sport created friendships across races, and this all seemed bad to him. Yet, he understood on a philosophical level that this was understandable, so here he was. He seemed glum. He then talked about his South African friends in great detail, one by one, what good guys they were and how well they treated him, with respect, more so than in the US. He was in pain, and this was a miserable day, cold wind, rain, standing for hours. So, we stood together. I always wondered if this schism in him hurt his heart. I tried to assuage his pain, but it was deep. We didn't talk much after that, but I think he liked my company as a fellow athlete.

For four years (1976-1980), I joined with Maud Russell, a 95-year-old sage who spent 40 years in China (for the YWCA), living in rural areas, and now published the Far Eastern Reporter. Writers like her, who had lived for many years in China, were provided an opportunity to publish their experiences. She edited each one of the articles, and all the writers appreciated it, including me. She got hit by a car near her residence on Riverside Drive in Manhattan a year earlier and broke her hip. She spent each day on a stationary bike in her apartment. Most older folks die at this age from this sort of accident. She was tough. Her books and manuscripts cluttered the apartment, meaning every few feet, walking through one room to another, one had to spin around in this labyrinth. No straight line. She had books and manuscripts piled high on the floor. I rearranged her apartment so that she could walk in a straight line and not hurt her hip.

Her best memory was in Mongolia, competing in a horse race across the plains, then climbing a butte, and back again to the start. She was over 60 at the time, and her white hair streamed in the wind, quite a sight, as she recalled, for black-haired Asians.

I worked for a year on the manuscript I submitted to her. She helped me contact the Chinese Sports Committee to get first-hand documents from them, which they translated for my study. We went over my manuscript line by line, which excited her very much.

By her suggestion, I wrote a history of sports in China during the twentieth century and the exclusion of China from the Olympics. The precursor to the Communist Party was the "New People's Study Society," which participated in physical culture.

As Mao said, "We also became ardent physical culturists. In the winter holidays, we tramped through the fields, up and down mountains, along city walls, and across streams and rivers. If it rained, we took off our shirts and called it a rain bath. When the sun was hot, we also duffed our shirts and called it a *sunbath*. In the spring winds, we shouted that this was a new sport called *'wind bathing.'* We slept in the open when frost was already falling, and even in November, we swam in the cold rivers. All this went under the title of *'body training.'* Perhaps it helped me a lot to build the physique that I needed so badly later on in my many marches back and forth across South China and on the Long

March back from Kiangsi to the Northwest." (Shinnick. Historical Perspective China and the Olympics. Far East Reporter 1978.)

The exclusion of China from the Olympics, or the two China policies, was engineered by a Chinese art collector, Avery Brundage, the head of the US Olympic Committee and a supporter of the German/American Nazi Bund. However, Nixon's Shanghai Agreement in 1972 endorsed the one-China policy, and this changed everything.

The announcement of China joining the Olympics in the fall of 1980 became a great victory for sports and also for the US/China People's Friendship Society. They held a big event, and the hall was crowded when we arrived. I picked Maud up at her apartment (we spent many hours together there) on 127th and Riverside Drive in New York City. She held my hand as we entered, and the crowd literally went wild when we appeared. They lifted her up onto a table so all could see her. I was pushed aside and stood in the corner. She introduced me, but no one looked; all eyes were on her. I was not offended; she was a jewel. I felt I had done good work; now, the Olympics would have the Soviets, China, and the US all in the Olympic games. I thought if the world saw these Cold War powers all together, then this could shift the constant Cold War rhetoric, a real vision of the world coming together.

This vision was shattered shortly. President Carter wanted to boycott the 1980 Moscow Olympics because the Soviets had crossed their own border into Afghanistan to protect the new socialist government against terrorist killings by Al-Qaeda/Taliban, mostly against women in the new government. The press was firing up the propaganda. I read all the objections about the US going to the Olympics. The Cold War drums were beating. I counted thirteen issues columnists were repeating against Moscow. Many things written did not jive with my first-hand knowledge while competing in Moscow in 1969. The real issue was Iran holding American hostages while demanding ransom, which was against State policy. Carter needed to seem strong.

I contacted Anniversary Tours, which had the right to arrange Olympic transportation, and got 21 free airline tickets to conduct a fact-finding tour. I recruited Olympians, sports activities, photographers, and writers. My idea was to interview ordinary citizens, and the Soviets gave us complete access and permission to interview anyone. Tracy Sundlun, whom I helped win the election for President of the Metropolitan Athletic Congress, became my right-hand person for this mission. The trip was set; all arrangements had been made in Moscow, with a side trip to Leningrad. Before we left, I was walking down a back street in Highland Park, New Jersey, heading to the store where I lived.

I had moved to Highland Park from Berkeley to accept a job at Rutgers. My 1972 tenure track position was changed to one of termination ending in 1980 because I took the fifth amendment in 1976 when subpoenaed to a grand jury looking into the location of Patty Hearst.

First in San Francisco, earlier that year, I was subpoenaed to a Grand Jury in San Francisco to name names of acquaintances in the Bay Area. I refused. When the US Attorney came into the room after my refusal, and I took the Fifth, he reached out with his hand to shake mine and said, "I have seen some of your competitions and wanted to meet you." On the way, he stepped into a wastebasket and clambered across the room with his foot in the basket. He let me go.

"I knew it," he said, "if I put you in jail, I assume you will never cooperate."

I said, "Never!"

This second one was then in Scranton, Pennsylvania. I did not feel I was under any obligation to incriminate myself or give names of associates. The government wanted me to be a stool pigeon to associates I met while at Berkeley. The board of governors said that they could not "countenance" my lack of cooperation and that I was an ideological dissident and had no place on the faculty of Rutgers. I was put on half-time pay. I waged a three-year legal struggle to get my full-time job back. I won back pay in return for giving up my tenured position. I had a choice, but three years at half-time were difficult with two kids, so I was vulnerable. This second grand jury wanted fingerprints, handwriting, and hair samples.

The FBI used the grand jury as a front for their investigation. They found one of her hideouts and wanted to tie me to it. Since I had never been to that hideout, I feared they would say after I gave them my hair samples that they found them in the farmhouse. They had my handwriting samples and fingerprints in my Air Force Officer's file. As for the hair samples, I asked the judge to hold them in his office and ask them to bring their samples to him for a match. After a six-month legal struggle, I was sent to Allenwood Federal Penitentiary in the fall of 1976.

The judge said, "You cannot determine the conditions of your cooperation."

I was released on January 19, in the winter of 1977, the day before Jimmy Carter was inaugurated. Carter let me go.

In 1980, a person walked up next to me (in Highland Park), matched my steps, and handed me a folder. He then disappeared. In the folder, there were details of a clandestine operation in Pakistan to destabilize the new progressive Afghanistan government.

A CIA agent would only have access to this classified information, I thought. I remembered Daniel Ellsberg, a CIA agent who had released secret Vietnam war information. So, it seemed plausible that this was an agent who wanted me to see what was really happening and probably disagreed with Carter's boycott.

Tracy had arranged for a meeting with the US Ambassador in Moscow, who had been President of IBM, and a friend of his father's, who owned Lear Jets. Before our noon meeting, we went to an Olympic gymnastics workout. Tracy could not pull himself away. I was antsy; we stayed for an hour too long and were already late. Plus, we needed to travel to the Embassy. We arrived over an hour late, and Tracy seemed unfazed. I felt we were insulting the ambassador. His wife scolded us, Tracy smiled at her, and he shifted the conversation to his father, who sent his greetings.

Things seemed fine, but something was on my mind from the information given to me, and I needed to be heard. I spilled the beans in one long oration. The secret police of Israel, Iran, and the US, through front businesses, had set up a camp in Pakistan to train insurgents, the Taliban/Al-Qaeda, to destabilize Afghanistan. This meant propaganda was brewing in the daytime to the civil society and terrorist attacks (mostly on women) on the elected progressive government, which had many women in key governmental posts, on the weekends.

Briefings in Moscow to our group purported that Afghanistan requested help thirteen times until they entered the country and that on weekends, women in power were assassinated on a large scale. The ambassador's wife lectured me and said, "This is entirely inappropriate to talk to my husband like this."

She raised her voice and tried to get me to leave.

The ambassador said, "Relax, honey. I like Phil. He is very much like me; he reminds me of my earlier self."

Pointedly, I asked him, "What if you were able to talk directly to Moscow on this issue? How long would it take to settle and get the athletes to the Moscow Olympic Games?"

He thought for a while and said, "I think I can get this done in three days."

He had conjured up a plan to appease both sides. He didn't tell me what, but I saw an opening and some light for the athletes. After the meeting, reporters were outside TASS, and one of them asked me, "How did it go?"

I replied, "There is some hope for the athletes to compete in the Olympics."

Our group went to construction sites and interviewed ordinary people about the thirteen anti-Soviet issues that the American news media were pushing. We took a short trip to Leningrad. As I came down the staircase from the aircraft onto the tarmac, an American official took me by the arm and said, "You have a phone call from the White House."

It was Phil Brown. He said to me, "You have created a hornet's nest in the White House."

Jody Powell and some others supported my stance, but some were adamant that the boycott should stand or the president would seem weak. I told Phil. "I did not talk about the armed training camp in Pakistan by Israel. The Shah, while naming the front companies and all the details, said that the ambassador thought he could settle it in three days if given permission to negotiate, so I expressed this as hope for the athletes."

Before we left to go back to the US, I realized we would have to tell the news media something about our trip. I called a meeting to go over a joint statement before landing at JFK Airport. I knew some of my friends were planning some mischief for laughs. So, the first thing in the meeting, I said, "Some of you have secrets you want to share with the group, and we must all be honest. How many of you have relations with the CIA?"

I was saying this as a joke. "Just raise your hand and speak up to our group."

Six people raised their hands and, one by one, told of their contacts with the CIA, who wanted them to report back to them. I thought this was okay; we had nothing to hide, plus the CIA had given me valuable information. I hammered out a joint statement from their comments and worked hard to satisfy everyone. Everyone then agreed on the statement, while ten agreed to attend the press conference. Others just wanted to go home after getting off the plane. So, the ten of us marched down the long terminal hallways at JFK.

At the end, we could see reporters. Tracy and I, as usual, were walking together, discussing our talks. When we got near, we looked around, and everyone had disappeared. I did not see any side doors, so they vanished into thin air. Into the bathrooms? It went well; we had detailed information on all the issues that were circulating before we left.

Back in Highland Park, I called Sports Illustrated (SI) and said I had a good story to report on our mission. They said they were not interested. I called the New York Times, but again, I was not interested. I sat glumly by the phone; the whole trip was being whitewashed. The phone rang. I remember that it might have been Sandy Padwe from SI. He said Carter sent a letter to all news media, saying that I was not to be trusted and that I broke US protocol on the trip. I picked up the phone next to me and called the *New York Times'* sports department and said I knew about the Carter letter and they were douchebags for the White House, they were nothing but lapdogs, they were a disgrace to journalism, and that I was going to call the senior editors and expose their complicity. I was pretty mad.

I got a call back from the *Times* in about 20 minutes. I could write the article; I had 30 minutes to call it to the editors for publication. I had no time to write it, yet I had hammered it out in my head from the group's response. It was all there in my head. I wrote nothing; I just recalled it from my memory, word by word, sentence by sentence.

The next day, I got half a page in the Times and pictures, but when I looked over the article, it made no sense; it was unreadable and incoherent. I examined it and saw they took the second sentence from the first paragraph, put it in the last paragraph, and vice versa, and scrambled the rest. I carefully cut the article line by line, put it back together, and then sent it to all the US news media, AP, UPI, etc. In a later edition of the Times, it was published exactly as I had called it.

Years later, I was at the Russian and Turkish Baths on Tenth Street in the East Village with the head of a world religious peace group, including the Pope, world religious, and state leaders. My world peace group, Athletes United for Peace, was a Non-Governmental Organization (NGO), and I met him at the UN. His response was laughter. I felt insulted and reminded him that this was not funny to me.

He said that in these instances where you go against US policy ideologically, they put you on ice, but as he said, "People like you are never deterred by this, so the next morning, they give you scrambled eggs for breakfast."

Tracy put on big meets at the Garden; he wore a tux and had all the officials in formal tuxedos as well. One by one, the officials came to him with problems. He would put his arm around them, say a few words, and off they would go to being officious; he had them all trained. US Track and Field for many years kept me on ice. Tracy had power, so she would tell me ways to get things done.

One year, the Soviet national team came to the Garden for a big indoor meet. The next night, they were to compete in the Meadowlands for a meet in New Jersey. It was freezing cold, and they waited outside their hotel room to be picked up; Cassell was in charge.

The ride never came, and they missed the meet, freezing themselves to death in the cold, waiting for the no-show ride. They wanted to go back home and would stay under one condition: I was put in charge of the Soviet team and took care of all matters. Tracy called to tell me this. I rented a van, took them shopping, sort of babysat for them, took care of minor complaints; they were all happy, being free in the city. I submitted the bill to Cassell, but he refused to pay, so I sued US Track and Field in small claims court. Tracy did not think much of it except that it was an inconvenience; he was the president of the NY track and field.

The lawyer for US T&F showed up, apologized to me, and made a weak defense, and the arbitrator gave me my expenses. Tracy thought this would happen. No big deal. Nothing was easy for me during these times. I expected it.

Chapter 27: Fourth of July in Idaho, in Cuba with the American Indian Movement and the Lake Placid Olympics, Measurement and Sport

During my childhood, in the late '40s and early '50s, on the Fourth of July, the Shinnick family went to Grangeville, Idaho, for Border Days. Covered wagons, palomino horses, a rodeo, and Kooskia, Kamiah, and Nez Perce Indians marched with bells and feathers up Main Street, pitching their tents on the parade grounds next to the rodeo grounds. The rodeo was central: Brahma Bull riding, calf roping, riding around barrels for time, and at night, fireworks unparalleled. I always had a fear that a Brahma bull would get me, so I sat up high in the stands in the corner.

One day, a Brahma jumped the rodeo fence and jumped up into the stands where I was sitting. My fear was happening; I was scared. The bull was four-legged and seemed to be headed towards me, but it stumbled, legs all crossed up on the bleachers. He hardly made any progress, so I ran down behind him, pretty close to him, as he was going up. He turned to the side and looked at me, one foot in one row of the bleachers and the other three legs all twisted up. He was pretty pathetic, not much of a threat to me, not in the grandstands. So, I slowly walked away, saying to myself, *It was not so bad. Clumsy bull.*

Left to right, Governors and wife Buttulsen, Clark, Nelson (my grandfather), and Gossett

My grandfather, Edwin Nelson, was Lt. Governor of Idaho and was driven up Main Street in the parade and around the rodeo grounds by the Police Chief. He waved to the crowd in his big Cadillac. All males had to grow beards (no beard, then you were put in neck shackles for two hours to have kids taunt you) and wear a six-gun in your holster for Border Days and rifles in holsters on their horse saddle. No cars were allowed in town, so everyone rode their horses from their ranches and farms and hitched them up on Main Street. Lots of messy horse poop on the street. Guns had to be given up entering a bar. One of my relatives got into a gunfight on Main Street after drinking; he shot a guy in the leg and went to jail.

In 1927, William Heiser was found in a snowdrift in a blinding blizzard, half-dead with a burst appendix, in pain and unable to move on the North/South highway. He was bringing his hogs to market. He was brought in by horseback by a farmer going by. Doc Shinnick (my grandfather was a surgeon) and Doc Weber operated on Heiser and afterward said, "He would have bled to death if he had not been half-frozen." They operated on the bar pool table.

I always got a bloody nose in the heat as a child; it would not stop, so my grandfather Nelson and the Police Chief took me home in a police car; the policeman put on his siren. I was lying down in the back, waiting for the blood to coagulate. I swallowed the blood down my throat. I wanted to look out; it was really bleeding. To inch up to look out, the crowd was parting and waving to my grandfather, Old Ed. He never talked much, but everyone seemed to love him.

At noon, all the kids lined up for races on Main Street in different age groups; winners got a silver dollar. My brother Nelson, my sister Susan, and I always won. On the third day of Border Days, all the farm kids and Native Americans knew I was fast, so they falsely started and were called back, but this did not deter them; they took off running before the gun again. No callback, so I took off running after their big head start and passed them in a whiz. They were not city kids used to running, and there was no real challenge. We called them clodhoppers. They rode tractors and horses. The Native Americans were a little faster.

During the '60s, I expressed my disgust with vitamins, anabolic steroids, uppers, and all sorts of performance-enhancing drugs that athletes were taking. It became too much for me, so I stopped all supplements. For 50 more years, I consumed only good food, no desserts, pop, or sweets. This lifestyle suited me well; I was rarely sick. In 1976, during one of my early peace trips to China, everyone got the flu except for my mother, me, and my morning running partner Alan Silber.

I was on my high horse against drug use by athletes and attended a 1978 World Tribunal at the World Youth Festival in Cuba. Socialist countries like massive youth activities, as I had seen in the Soviet pioneer camps or the World University Games. I got a place on the agenda of the World Tribunal and was sequestered in a room, waiting for my turn to discuss athlete doping. The room was fairly large, and in the far corner, I saw five or six Native Americans, mostly from Pine Ridge, waiting to testify. They were about the size of my buddy, discus thrower friend Al Pemberton, way over ' and muscular and fierce-looking. I had nothing to say to them or them to me, so I stayed my distance.

After about 6 hours, things lightened up. I think they had been rehearsing their testimony. Slowly, they got nearer, and one came over. The conversation flourished. I had traveled around the US, and as a historian, I gained access to the archives in the basement of Native American museums. I was looking for objects of sport. I found leather balls, lacrosse sticks, etc. I knew that history and talked about it. Beyond that, my Olympian feats created closeness; also, I had no fear of any man, and they could sense that. One was a Five Nation of the Iroquois Nation, an Onondagan member, and the others from Pine Ridge, or Oglala Lakota. The Onondaga member invited me to upstate New York.

I drove north, arrived, and found the place to meet. We had some tea and learned of the Akwesasne newspaper, which I wrote for. We had an idea: the Lake Placid Olympics were approaching, and why not display the traditional sport of the Iroquois as a cultural display? We thought this would be good for the Olympic movement and also educate the local people about the richness of Native American winter sports. My interest in measurement and obsession with numbers needed a closer look at the origins of sport. The soccer boundary stretched miles, with no referees. Athletes understood their limits and how to behave. The timing for the start or finish was dictated by sunrise, sunset, harvest, funerals, marriages, treaties, and important events.

One winter sport I liked involved a log that was dragged and then wetted for a slick surface. A woman would run along the round opening and throw a spear; the winner would be the one who slid it the furthest. Snow snaking. Alex de Tocqueville, in his Encyclopedia, defined democracy as the summer gathering of the Five Nations of the Iroquois to resolve all disputes, which took all summer; rarely were these settlements violated after a complete hearing. A delegation went to the Lake Placid Winter Olympic organizers pitching the idea, mostly to deaf ears, yet they persisted.

Meanwhile, progressives in the area discovered that the Olympic Village was to be converted into a prison. Their argument centered around, first, a violation of the Olympic spirit, and next, those who would be imprisoned were mostly from New York City, miles away from their families, and difficult to visit. They deemed it a stupid idea. I met these Olympic prison protesters or organizers, and my Iroquois friends learned of their efforts and were also interested.

Meeting with the Lake Placid Olympic organizers went nowhere, and our proposal had no effect. The organizers contacted the press, and it became an issue. I got a call from my Onondaga friend saying there was a big problem. Chief Thompson had been arrested; local police, either local or state, came onto the reservation, cut down a swath of trees on the reservation, and built a fence. They wanted to fence them in on their own land. This was clearly a violation of the Sovereignty of the Nation, a treaty violation. These police had no rights on their land.

We all knew the real issue. Pine Ridge (The American Indian Movement) made all police nervous they would have another incident to sully their Olympic plans. They overreacted, violated Treaty rights, and had no authority to arrest Thompson on his own land. This was a legal issue, and over the next year, I spent my time reading the legal briefs for Thompson and organizing a defense for him with the Center for Constitutional Rights, the group that defended me (Morton Stavis) in all my legal troubles with the government.

It all worked out, and I published its history in the Journal of Ethnic Studies, titled "The Sovereignty Rights of the Mohawks, Natural Sport, and the Olympic Prison."

In Cuba with Javier Sotomayor, World Record Holder High Jump

Taylorism, or the measurement of work motions and time, became the cloak that sports officials saw as the direction of sport: more rules, more boundary restrictions, precise timing, more officials to judge, and scientifically manufactured drugs for higher performance. The sport had lost its roots in natural cycles, and instead of the athlete as the center of events, a rule could negate an action. For example, a jump shot from the corner but toe on the line, or after the clock time, was negated, so the truth of an athlete's action depended upon strict boundaries and time. An action such as a jump shot or jumping a fraction over the board meant no jump, more technology, and less human judgment. A feat depended upon a rule, not so much about whether the shot was made. So, the truth of an action depends not on the act but on how it fits within the rules. The essence of sport is to deny reality or truth.

Chapter 28: A Guest of the US Marshall in Allenwood Penitentiary, on the Prison Basketball Team, New President Carter Frees Me, 1977

January 19, 1977, Allenwood Federal Penitentiary

A messenger came by my cot and said, "The Warden wants to talk with you."

I had one of hundreds of cots set up in a large open space. I had a single bed and a light stand in about a 5' space. My books were tucked under my cot. This was my home for the last three months as a guest of the US Marshal for refusing to give up my hair samples to a Grand Jury, which the FBI was using as a front for their investigation into the kidnapping of Patty Hearst. They had found one of her hideouts in Pennsylvania, a place I had never been to, and I thought if I gave my samples, they would say they found them at the hideout. I asked the Federal Judge to oversee comparisons, and he ruled that I could not set up conditions and thus was in federal contempt. I took the Fifth Amendment.

(Left) At the Federal Court in Scranton, Pennsylvania. Taking the Fifth Amendment and was sent to Allenwood as a guest of the US Marshal for contempt. Quincey Shinnick, Jay Weiner, Shannon Shinnick, and Shinnick. (Right) Rutgers students protesting

The warden said, "I got a call from the White House."

Jimmy Carter was being inaugurated at the time. The warden added, "The government is not interested in you anymore. You can go home."

I said, "Tomorrow morning. I have a big basketball game tonight."

During my first few weeks in detention, my cot was put in the hallway near the back door. Inmates liked to go out for a smoke, and when they did, the north wind and snow came onto my cot.

Down the hall, inmates watched television, sometimes all night. The structure was all cinder blocks; the TV was in a cubicle, and it was difficult to hear (ricocheting off the walls), so the sound was turned up even though the inmates were only feet away. The sound bounced off the outside wall and into my ears as if I were next to the loud TV. I felt this was my torture, and my job was not to get rattled. I did not sleep much; I got my training with two young girls, and I never slept through the night.

Gordon Liddy had been thrown in prison for the dirty deeds of Watergate. Each morning after my run, Liddy would sit at my breakfast table. I never spoke to him. He told authorities that they should have armed guards at Allenwood, which upset the inmates. This prison was for those on the way out after being in maximum security prisons. The inmates were not there to escape. They took Lindy's cot outside my door into the snow drifts and set it on fire.

Everyone knew I would, under no conditions, cooperate with authorities. When I entered Allenwood, demonstrators could be heard outside, and inmates inside went on a two-day hunger strike out of solidarity with me. I had a beard and long hair. It had to be cut, but I was there because I would not give hair samples. The inmates devised a way, and the warden agreed with the inmates' plan. I stripped down to just my shorts. An inmate had been a barber, so he cut my hair, and afterward, he swept it all up into the toilet. Dusted me off, then swept the floor again many times.

One by one, inmates came and sat on my cot in the hall while I was reading. When I paused and looked up, each told their story. I learned about the frame-ups, injustices, and their crimes in great detail. The gangsters liked to gather around my cot and talk business, the new silencers for guns, and news from the outside. Everyone felt safe around me to say anything; I was like a confessor. I felt at home. I had never had so much respect in the last few years.

The first few days there, the weather was cold, 10 degrees, with a blizzard and storming, so I went out for a run before the sun came up. I wore a warm hat and gloves, with a scarf around my waist, and out I went with my friend Jay Weiner, a reporter from Newsday. He had received a similar subpoena and requested hair samples, fingerprints, and writing samples. The wind was over 20 MPH, and we entered a blizzard; the road was pure ice, and the snow swirled without settling. I liked it; Jay and I just let ourselves go forward into the wind, which held us up. It seemed effortless. We could not see more than twenty feet ahead when a large truck appeared. Inmates could volunteer for farm work, and they were hanging onto the side of the truck.

As they got near and saw us out in the blizzard, the truck stopped, and they gawked. They wore ten layers of clothes and clumsy boots. These inmates could volunteer for farm duty, milking the cows and feeding them. They were driving back and came for breakfast. They went by.

I felt good, and then a sharp pain struck my abdomen; it was so painful that I went off the road and ended up curled up in the snow, unable to move from the pain. The realization that I was put on half-time at Rutgers labeled an ideological dissident and now in prison made my future seem bleak. After the terms of the grand jury were up next summer, I was facing another 18 months in prison. I could not move, but I felt comfortable in the snow— not moving. In the fetal position, I felt no pain.

A cow came over to me, curious about who I was. She stuck her nose near me to get a good look. Her nose was moist, and steam came out of her nostrils. She seemed comfortable in the blizzard. She came near my face, and her tongue flipped out across my cheek. I got the message: "What is this fuss about? We are alive and well. Did she know I was a cowboy and liked her?"

I stood up, and the pain left. Near the end of the road was a left turn, so we ran up to the barn, where I saw the haystack and the milking area. Some of the inmates were throwing out hay to the other cows and looked up and waved. So, it was big news that we were out early in the morning.

The warden said, "We could run to the church, which was about a mile and a half away, and turn around but not run beyond that or go to the barn. I suppose they thought we could just run away, but where?"

Months later, I still adhered to my routine: a good run, some weightlifting, and three square meals a day. I spent most of my time reading. One day, the innate coach of the prison basketball team approached me and asked me, "Do you want to play?"

I responded, "Not tonight. I ran 6 miles, lifted some weights, and now my belly is full from dinner. Maybe tomorrow."

He replied, "You either come to practice, or you are not on the team."

"You're a lousy coach and not concerned about my health," I said to him.

"I can't be on your team with your attitude," I added and then walked away.

After practice, some of the players came to me and asked, "What happened?"

I told them, "I'm not interested in playing for that coach. He has no authority over me. He was asking me to practice on a full stomach and after two hard workouts."

Later, they returned and said they had fired him, and we had a new coach. The next day, I went to practice. Being in top shape, I dunked the ball backward and forward and was ready to practice. When I came in for a regular layup, it spun off the rim and dropped to the floor. The new coach came over to me and said, "Go run laps for missing the layups."

I said, "I do not run for punishment. I run for fun. I like running." I went over to the bench, untied my shoes, and started to walk out. The practice stopped; everyone looked at me.

As I started for the door, the coach ran after me and apologized, saying, "Sorry, you can stay. You don't have to run laps."

I then became the center of defense, guarding the paint. On offense, I alternated from low to high post.

1976: At 33, a one-step dunk playing in Allenwood

The night of the big game was hours after the Carter reprieve. I could go home, but the big game was important to me. The local team came into the gym. The stands were full, perhaps with over 300 inmates. The local team was all white, and we were black, except for me. The average height was taller than any of us; I judged the average height to be about 6' 8". I am 6' 4" and the tallest on our team.

We had good players! Yet, as I looked carefully at them, they appeared to be around 25 or 26 years old and seemed to be former college players. They were slightly flabby and out of shape but had great skills. I knew they would be easy to tire and could be beaten. My teammates just stared at them. I found out later they were scared to death.

I outjumped their center on the tip to control the ball for the setup. A player fumbled my tip, and then no one could hit a shot; they were flat-footed on defense. The other team sensed this clumsiness, got the ball, and a big forward faked out our wing defense and charged the basketball right down the center lane at me. I moved up to meet him and wondered about his alacrity. He charged fast, so I chest-butted him as he drove, going up for his shot, which he thought would be easy. He hit the floor hard, and I knocked the wind out of him, and he got the charge. I made my foul shots. This repeated all half; I out-rebounded them and threw the ball out for fast breaks, but my teammates could not handle the ball. I made all the points, nearly 20. The score at the half was 21 to 47.

The heat from the crowd, along with the heat turned up for the game in winter, meant it was 85 degrees in the gym. I was melting, not used to the heat from my morning runs. My jersey was too tight, and I could hardly breathe, tired from running the court full blast. At half-time, I was panting and ripped my jersey down the side to open my chest. I had a gallon of water in a glass jug and knew I had to cool myself down. I started to drink it all.

The coach looked over at me, sweating, sitting on the floor against a wall. I could hardly breathe, totally exhausted, and trying to recover. He wondered how I could survive the second half.

He started in on my teammates, saying, "You're all a disgrace. You're prisoners, and you all act as if you have no heart. What happened to you? Is your humanity gone? You're a bunch of losers, but I know all of you, and in my heart, I know what you're capable of doing."

He continued, "Look at Shinnick. Every minute, he plays hard with no fear. He can hardly stand up; he's done. What is it you are afraid of? We're all prisoners, but we're more than all that. These guys can be defeated. Look at me. What is wrong with you guys? Now is the time to get over whatever it is that makes you afraid. Big white guys? You must show what you are made of. I'm a prisoner too, but is that all you are, and you are not more? I know what you can do. I feel this deep in my heart, and we can be proud of ourselves. I want all of you to go out there and show your stuff. Your heads are up your ass, and I am ashamed of how you played this first half."

Something came over my teammates. I could feel it. They kept looking at me. I was a wreck, still breathing hard. I looked pathetic. Each patted me on the shoulder as they went out to the floor and charged out.

I never got the ball, except for my rebounds, but then I threw it out. This time, all my teammates ran the court, hit all their shots, and took all the burden away from me. The other team was out of shape and tired. No one charged the center since they knew they would get hit hard by me. The inmates in the crowd went wild. They stayed on their feet the entire second half, and players' names were being chanted. With each swish, there was hooting, hollering, and taunting of the other team, who seemed to be in a trance.

We were not making any mistakes, and they could hardly get a shot up on defense. Yet, they had good skills and had to shoot from the outside. They missed often, and we got their rebounds. My teammates were outplaying me, and I was not needed. It felt like they were saying, "You did the first half; this half is ours."

We lost by two points, 99 to 97, but to the very end, we kept surging. The crowd did not care about the score, only the fantastic spectacle before their eyes.

After the game, all the inmates came onto the floor and hugged all the players. The coach was lifted up. Game over. The other team was in shock. I went back to my cot, still fatigued, but I was so happy that my teammates not only did not pass the ball to me but also took over defense for me.

Everyone made points, and most had lifetime bests: they had a game. I walked by the phone area, and the coach was talking to his wife. In tears, he was saying, "Honey, at half-time, I am not sure where it came from, but I talked to my inmates and berated them for not giving their best, asking them whether their incarceration had made them into stupid, heartless people. I knew each of them and knew they could do better. Somehow, I lit a fire inside them and transformed them. It's the single best thing I've ever done in my life. I now feel capable of really doing anything. I'm different, and I'm so much in love with you and so grateful to my inmates."

Then, he sobbed and sobbed in pure joy as his players walked by, and each gave reverence to him and touched him in the most respectful way. They put their hand on his shoulder, paused, but said nothing.

The coach continued talking to his wife, "Honey, my inmates love and respect me, and I put a torch under their butts. I've never seen such a high-quality basketball. They were on fire; each and every person, and even the bench, couldn't miss. We skunked them real good. I am so happy."

I left the next morning at 6 AM, not telling anyone I was leaving. Before I went to bed, the whole prison was buzzing, and fans gathered around each player, going over how good they played and talking about minute details of their play. The players kept saying, "Did you see that?"

"Yes, yes, yes, you did well."

Hugs and high-fives were all around.

Chapter 29: Playing Baseball in Nicaragua in the Warzone, Fire on the Prairie, and Firefighting in the Idaho Mountains

Mid-1980s Nicaragua

Carter had been defeated, presumably because he could not free the American hostage in Iran. This led to Ronald Reagan being elected, who assured everyone that he could release prisoners while not violating US policy with no ransom. He did pay ransom to the Iranians in weaponry and money, and it is not clear what he gave them beyond that. Drug trafficking money was freed up to fund the counter-revolutionary force in Nicaragua, the Contra.

Guy Benjamin, a Stanford and SF Forty Niners quarterback and now director of Athletes United for Peace after my four-year turn, organized this trip. We were in a Contra prison camp and played the Contras in a softball game. Soviet-manufactured helicopters flew overhead in circles.

It was in an open field, and behind the catcher's box was the prison, which was more like an apartment complex with no fences. I was the pitcher. I liked pitching and had mastered it in grade school; I spun with my wrist, so the ball went off the bat haywire, changing up the speed without the batter knowing it. I speeded up my arm on the wind-up, but just before release, I froze, which slowed the pitch down.

Michael James, a former football player, a Chicago progressive, actor, radio announcer, and writer, was catching. He held AUP road races in Chicago. Guy was in the left outfield.

In the far outfield was a grass fire, about two feet high, burning in a line eighty yards in length. I could smell it while keeping my eye on it. I did not know who started it or why it was still burning. In 1961, Charlie Miller, on his ranch, drove his truck across the hayfield at 60 MPH toward me as I was bucking bales of hay, slammed on the brakes, and jumped out. His face darkened with soot. He seemed spooked.

"Phil, I need you to drive my other truck over there,"

Pointing to his grandfather's house 200 yards away.

"In the back is a 50-gallon barrel of diesel with a pump."

He pointed in the direction of smoke.

"I am on my CAT making a fireline, and it is low on fuel. I cannot get stuck near the fire, or I will lose the CAT. I want you to go in a straight line to the fire. If a fence is in your way, go right through it and over the stream, and I will meet you there. Now!"

He sped away in the opposite direction to the highway. I ran to the pickup with 50 gallons of diesel in the back. I took off as fast as I could go across the fields, came to a fence, speeded up, and went right through it. I saw a stream ahead; I knew it to be about four feet deep with a sharp bank on the other side.

I hesitated, then leaped the bank into the stream, but the truck was sinking into the stream, so I put it in reverse and sped up the stream bank backward onto the flat. I kept it in reverse till I had some room to go faster. I gunned it all out and flew off the bank almost to the other side, and as it hit the bottom, I gunned it again forward and went up the other bank. The weight of the diesel helped in the mud. Charlie Miller was waiting for me, and the smoke was thick.

"Take my truck and go back the way you came; this is dangerous."

Later that night, he came back, and I asked him what happened. He said that the fire came closer to him, and he put the steering on the CAT in a locked position to go in circles, and then he ran.

The next morning, we went to see what happened to the CAT; it was in the center of the field, stalled out and safe, a miracle! The wind died, and the fire abated.

The next week after hay season, Paul Swift and I went to Coeur d'Alene, Idaho, and signed up for fire fighting in the Selkirk mountain range. It took us all night to get to the fire; while still dark, we climbed the side of the mountain as the sun rose.

Firefighters told stories, one after the other, of the wind picking up and fire tree topping while trapping fighters inside the fire. We got to the fire, which was about 6" high and burning slowly. With our shovel, we just made a fireline by throwing dirt on the fire and stopping it. Yet, old logs were still burning, which had to be cut up.

In our softball game, Guy was on the left field, and behind him, the fire burned and glowed. Smoke was in the air! He was instructing my pitching. I think he wanted me to let them hit the ball so he could catch it and play. I did not want to give up a hit.

As a quarterback, he was used to giving orders. I ignored Guy; he got steamed up, and we exchanged mad glances. He then came storming from the left field toward me. So, I dropped the ball and charged him. We chest-butted, but I got my arms around his arms, pinned him, and spun him around. He is 6' 4", about 220 lbs.

When this happened, we realized how absurd this was. We were at odds in the middle of a softball game with the Contras. We sort of laughed because we were very good friends, and I went back to pitching.

James and I had figured it out! We had hand signals for fast or slow, up or down, or inside and outside. I had control, so this worked well, and the batters were off guard. I wanted to pitch a no-hitter. James was in the catcher's stance; he had a pair of running shorts on, the elastic in the legs was overstretched, and there he was with his testicles hanging down.

So, he calls out, "Two balls!" The whole Contra team laughed, so he had to keep putting them back often, but no one minded after that.

My turn came up to bat. The Contra's pitcher did not like to throw me anything good since I got a few ground hits off him. He threw one of those very high pitches, which dropped from the sky before the plate; this one went too far over the plate. Like swatting a fly on the high wall, I jumped up and hit it squarely.

The ball flew high and then disappeared; my ball got airborne and disappeared from the updraft of the fire. It landed near the fire, a home run. We saw no sign of the Sandinista; I think the Contras were not interested in running away and were good sports. The helicopters were ominous. Why the fire?

We traveled further into the warzone where the Contras were making raids. We stayed at a farmer's commune, where they were all packing pistols. We played in a cow pasture, which had deep ruts from hooves in the spring mud. I pitched but kept looking up to the ridge which overlooked our field.

We were all nervous; we played the farmers, and they were good ball players. I think Guy influenced me instead of not letting the Contras hit. Like before, I felt it was okay to give these farmers easy pitches. Running the bases meant high kneeing, watching not to break an ankle.

In Managua, before we drove up to the warzone, our group met with the leadership of the Sandinistas in the dining area of our hotel.

One of the Sandinistas turned to me and said, "Phil, we caught a Contra in a tree outside your room last night with a bomb. He was going to bomb the power station."

A movie producer sat with our group and asked Guy, James, and me to be part of a movie being made about William Walker. Walker was an outsider who joined the revolution, waging an unauthorized war, and became president. We were to run down a hill with weapons at full speed. I liked the idea! I was used to running fast downhill from my Berkeley days in Strawberry Canyon.

In the end, I put a thumbs down on the plan because we were on a mission. I regretted this, thinking how fun it would be as James was an actor and we would have created a great scene.

Eventually, Nancy Reagan finds out about Ronnie's deal, and he has to make a confession. I always wondered what it was that caused the US to overthrow the progressive government of Iran and put the Shah in power, kill the president of Chile, destabilize Afghanistan, do dirty deeds in Africa, become obsessed with socialism, and support subversion through the world against progressives.

From my experience, I also saw counterforces within our government exposing some of the more egregious plots, like Daniel Ellsberg and the Pentagon Papers.

Chapter 30: A Peace Mission to Greece and the Olympic Torch, Finding My Direction through Meditation, Swimming in Cold Water, Another Greek Peace Mission and the Lake Placid Olympics, A UN Peace Mission, Medicine Saved Me

1982 Olympia Greece

Charlene Mitchell and Mike Myerson headed the US Peace Council, a progressive organization in New York City that had ties to international peace organizations. Charlene was the first Black woman to campaign for the US president in 1968 under the Communist Party.

She told me that Melina Mercouri, the then-current Minister of Culture and Sport in Greece, who had previously been ostracized from Greece under the junta, said that the Greeks had created an Olympic Torch of Peace to rally against the proliferation of nuclear arms between the Soviet Union and the US.

She asked me, as a US Olympian, if I could come and speak at peace rallies. Both Charles and Melina knew of my efforts to organize and conduct sports events between the Soviet Union and the US to foster friendship between the two nations.

When I arrived in Greece at the airport, local peace activists picked me up. I had two small bags, one containing my passport, wallet, and address book. A peace worker picked up my bigger bag and then carried it to his car's truck, motioning for me to get into his car.

As I was walking to his car, another person reached for my shoulder bag and said, "Your transport car truck is full, so I will take it in my car." He said this while pointing to a car parked in front of my transport.

I resisted! He pulled my shoulder bag off my shoulder and put it in his car truck along with other luggage. Although abrupt, It seemed to me that this was a friendly gesture to help. When I arrived at the hotel, I went to the car, but my bag was missing. The person who took my bag, disguised as a peace worker, was not there. I then had no passport, money, or wallet with credit cards to start my mission. The young peace workers pooled their money and gave me just enough money to get by.

Early the next day, I went to the Pantheon and was greeted by Minister Mercouri. She rushed over to me and then gave me a hug as our whole bodies were pressed together, from the tip of our toes to our cheeks. It was probably the kindest, warmest hug I had ever gotten while holding it for some time. She kissed me on the cheek on both sides, held my hand, and took me over to some dignitaries she pointed to.

As we walked, she talked about her marriage to Julius Dassin, who had been Blacklisted in the US and fled. She discussed her many years living outside of Greece and was so happy to see me. She seemed to whisper as her body was pressed to mine side to side. She seemed almost in tears. I think she wanted to tell me I was not alone in this world, that there were others like me. She wanted to comfort me. Then, she introduced me to the mayor of Athens and the president of the University of Athens.

Both were very friendly, and the president said he had arranged for me to give a series of lectures the next day at his University of Athens. Melina did not let go of my hand during the press conference. They all discussed the route of the peace torch through Europe and Canada, then to the UN, and to a peace rally in Central Park. It was an ambitious plan! Minister Mercouri said next week was the first day of spring. Throughout Greece at high noon, the whole nation will stop and give 5 minutes of silence in tribute to Mother Earth for her gift. It was our duty to preserve it.

My small support group drove me north to the Balkans, where there was to be a peace rally at the stadium where a martyred long jumper had won the Balkan championship. I was to be one of the key speakers along with the poet laureate of Greece. The full stadium held 50,000 here, and half the stadium was full of young peace activists.

An elevated podium faced the stands. There was a podium with a microphone and a translator. I talked about my 1968 Athens competition at the Council of Sport Military (NATO), which I won. I felt a shroud over me because of the junta and how sad I was. My schoolboy days taught me an understanding of democracy, and my Greek readings shaped my political vision.

ΠΑΓΚΟΣΜΙΑ ΕΙΡΗΝΟΔΡΟΜΙΑ
ΟΛΥΜΠΙΑ • ΑΘΗΝΑ • Ν. ΥΟΡΚΗ
15.5.82 • 16.5.82 • 7.6.82

"Today, I see before me the ancient spirit of peace and freedom that was missing when I competed in Athens. This fills my heart with appreciation for what I see before me today: my true comrades in peace, my real brothers and sisters. I feel this today and am so happy."

A spectator in the front row stood up on the railing waving a large blue flag, turned to the crowd and shouted something, then jumped onto the track, and the whole crowd emptied the stands. They did not go single file but jumped over the railings like ants swarming onto the field and circled the fields on the track. Banners flying high, a true revolutionary spirit resounded!

1982 flag-waving Greek Peace Activists

I sat down. I thought to myself that person is their real leader, and it is him they are responding to, not me. With flags waving, they chanted, "The people united will never be defeated in Greek."

In China years ago, I read the poetry of Mao, who wrote about the Long March. They waved flags and sang songs of solidarity as they marched west, much like I saw here. I was not finished with my speech, and this person interrupted it. I felt dejected and felt I came all this way to not be heard. I hardly looked up, but I heard them chanting.

The Greek poet laureate, Yannakis Potamitis, who sat several chairs away, stood up and then stood in front of my chair.

"What is wrong?" I told him.

He replied, "Phil, they are chanting for you! Look at them; they are on fire with appreciation that you understood them."

I later talked about that martyred long jumper who gave his life for peace, and I was proud to be giving him homage, which he so deserved.

I then spoke again, "They killed him on his motorcycle, gunned him down all for his outspoken freedom talk. People who stand up for peace are themselves in danger, but today, we are free to speak our peace. We are free! I learned of democracy from my high school Latin teacher, and my heroes were Achilles, Apollo, and the great Olympians of Zeus while avoiding Ajax's fate of suicide for not getting the shield of Achilles and feeling dishonored. We fight for honor, but a peaceful culture is more important. This framed my life, and today, I see that legacy before me."

After the speeches, this red-headed Greek poet, Yannakis, sat next to me high up in the stands next to Melina and local leaders. I pointed to a large scaffolding to the side of the stadium and people with cameras pointed at us.

"I see no work being done around here. Who are those people on the scaffolding, and what are they doing up there?"

He leaned over and said, "Phil, they are spying on you, and I think they are the CIA. The crowd senses that and also knows the sacrifices you have made for peace."

He looked over at the scaffolding while scribing a poem.

Life had been difficult for me in the US, but here, I felt real love and appreciation. So new to me!

Several years later, I went to another Los Angeles Olympic Torch lighting ceremony in Olympia, and this one had a good outcome. I returned to Athens to get a new passport and airline tickets, which were lost. This took days! That night in Athens was my last, and I had an early flight out the next morning.

Near dawn, I did my usual early morning meditation while lying in bed. Almost real, I heard the voice of one of my children calling for me. I was in a ranch-style house that had a soft rug with a split level. The voice came from the lower level; I was very excited to see my child. I jumped down the four steps onto the lower level with glee. I had momentum but stopped when I saw a pitch-black barrier across half of the room.

I heard a voice say, "Stop, or you are dead."

I froze, and a terror came over me like I had never experienced. Fear is not my thing, yet this paralyzed me! My first thought was that I should not have stopped my momentum but continued, put my foot high up on the opposite wall, and somersaulted backward into the room and up the stairs. I opened my eyes in terror and saw the window open and the curtain flapping. I stood up, went into the bathroom, and looked at myself in the mirror. I was ashen white, and my eyes were like I had seen a ghost. I felt unglued. I gathered my things and quickly took a taxi to the airport, but halfway there, I realized I left my passport and ticket in my room.

I went to a retreat center for progressives in the mountains of upstate New York in an attempt to understand what this fear was all about. Only about 30 people were at the lodge, having small group discussions on the lawn with folding chairs and discussing situations around the world with foreign guests. I did not attend. I went to a lake nearby and sat on a flat rock while meditating on the space above the lake.

After about half an hour, I could see the space above the water had texture and direction; it was like a plasma, and each day, it changed directions, like snowfall. This was very pleasing to me; I felt I was not alone. I could see nature's wonders in space.

On the third day, while sitting on the rock, a long black snake came up out of the water and slivered up to me, then coiled up and looked at me. I was not scared; it was not poisonous and harmless.

On the ranch, I came across many rattlesnakes, and I simply reached down and grabbed their tail, snapped them like a whip, and broke their neck. This was a nice snake. It looked at me for some time, and I did not move; it turned away and slivered into the water again. A thought occurred to me: *My greatest fear is drowning in cold water!*

This lake was very cold, so I did not swim in it. I stood up and followed the snake into the lake, which chilled me. I could only swim for twenty yards along the shore before I needed to swim back.

Each day, I followed the shoreline to the direction of the snake. I figured out that if I watched my breath and ignored the cold, I could stay in much longer. Finally, I headed straight across the lake but had to turn back.

With every passing day, I got a little further. Then, finally, I decided to swim across the lake and back, but not for one second could I think of the cold and only my inhalation and exhalation. If I lost concentration, I would drown. I did it! I overcame my greatest fear. That snake was really my good friend; I could sense it.

In the afternoon, I did a closed-eye meditation (Zazen) on the rock, and after about half an hour, I entered a great abyss. It was a great expanse and seemed to go on forever in all directions, but I could sense a vibration, sort of like a cloud, not white or dark but in between.

Far off, I could see a black spot coming toward me. As it got nearer, I could see it was a man in a black tuxedo and top hat, cane, and white gloves. He whirled the cane and tap-danced toward me like a vaudeville act. I watched him carefully. When he came near me, he tipped his hat; it rolled down his arm into his hand.

We both looked at the hat, and then he looked up at me in my eyes and said, "You want enlightenment? Go to medicine." Then, he vanished.

I stopped my retreat and went home. As I entered my Highland Park house, the phone rang. It was Robert Wood Johnson Hospital. A group of physicians wanted me to come in for a meeting. I had some contact with some of these doctors since I had been teaching a course at Rutgers on the sociology of health. I immediately went to the hospital and entered a room with five white coats.

They said they all got the same message, that I could help them with patients who did not do well in surgery. Would I help them? They wrote a prescription to see this patient. I would be paid (1984 Cervical Laminectomy C 2–8, anterior fusion C 6–7, infected wound, skin grafts, C 8 right and left motor sensory limitations). I met with this construction worker, and he had a hole in the back of his neck.

It seemed they changed the hospital rules; patients could not be in the hospital for over three days for these sorts of operations. They discharged him, and his sutures broke open. They could not repair it and used pig skin to cover the large hole. I figured out the problem.

Day after day, he was standing in an open building with a cold breeze on his back while checking off construction materials. His tissue had hardened. I simply used electrical stimulation and my fingers to gently loosen up the tissue. He was paralyzed, and all movement came back in ten days. These doctors then came back to me and said they could not teach me anything, and I had to go to New York for training.

My referral was a physician and researcher on the State Board of Medicine. He respected the recommendation of these well-known New Jersey doctors, and I was accepted into the medical training of physicians. I did not have an MD degree, so I was put on a research protocol. I then could do non-drug physical medicine without an MD degree with my Ph.D. and research background as an equivalent. I joined medical societies as the only non-MD and got an inside view of medicine.

Eventually, I became an assistant professor at New York Medical College, as well as a faculty member at an international college. Later, I passed the national exam for a license in Chinese medicine without going to an acupuncture school, as recommended by the head of the Rusk Institute, Mathew Lee, MD.

Weeks later, after my retreat, I heard a knock on my door in New Jersey. Standing on the porch was a young male who had my bag, which had been stolen from me in Athens. He said he did not know anything about it, only that he had been given the job to deliver it to my house. I went through my bag and could see what they were after; my address book had all my contacts in many countries as well as political contacts in the US. The only thing missing was some dried magic mushrooms that were given to me.

Later the next evening, I got a call before I went to bed that the Peace Torch had arrived in Montreal, and 80,000 people showed up in a stadium for a peace celebration that the torch inspired. The problem was they were prohibited from bringing it into the US bound for the UN by immigration officials.

It appeared that this torch was a danger to the Cold War politics of nuclear proliferation. We devised a plan! I was to take a plane out of LaGuardia, disembark, get the torch, and then get on a plane back to New York at the next gate, leaving in 10 minutes.

The big problem was that the plane was to leave LaGuardia in just over an hour, and I had to drive to the airport, at least a 45-minute drive. There was a driving rainstorm. I had a Land Cruiser with a four-wheel drive, so I drove like a madman to the airport and just made the flight.

When I got off the plane, the peace workers were waiting for me. They had a blanket they wrapped around the torch and two cans of fuel, one diesel, and the other kerosene, in a backpack. I quickly grabbed these and got instructions on how to light the torch. One fuel was for smoke to be seen from a long distance, the other for fire for close-up viewing.

When I got home, I realized that the government did not want this torch in the US, so I locked all the doors to my house, locked myself in a room, and hardly slept, lying next to the torch with my arm around it.

The next morning, I headed for the UN, and on the way, I saw a field with plaster of Paris figures for gardens and spotted a bird bath, which I bought. Going into the shop, I saw an urn that looked Grecian, and I also bought it. At the UN, I set up the bird bath, put the urn on top, and filled the urn full of fuel with rags to keep it burning.

Buddhist monks from around the world had walked for months chanting peace prayers and had arrived just in time at the UN for this ceremony. Native-American shamans with full headdresses had also come from many tribes. They all surrounded the fire in the urn; the monks beat their drums as did the Native Americans and threw incense in the fire, chanting prayers of peace.

Mario Cuomo had supported senior citizen health days in Central Park, which I helped organize, and was a supporter of sport and peace. He had been a professional baseball player. We gave him the honor to hold the peace torch, and we marched up Fifth Avenue with the torch flaming to enter the park. I was amazed at his strength; he held the torch high up in front of him, and wondered how he could do it for so long.

In Central Park, this was the largest peace gathering in history, with all the top performers in the world there, including the Rolling Stones. When the people lined the street on the way, I added more kerosene for a good flame, but into Central Park, I put more diesel so that all those gathered could see the smoke as we entered the park.

The crowd roared with approval as they spotted the smoke, and the music began. I immediately went home to rest, pretty frayed. Guy Benjamin, a Stanford and 49er quarterback, took over my job as director of Athletes United for Peace so I could enter medicine full-time. My life had changed!

Chapter 31: Initiated at the Altar of Zeus as an Olympian Peacekeeper, Soviet Athletes Vote Not to Come to the LA Olympics Over Reagan Not Guaranteeing Their Safety

1984 Olympia Greece—Another Peace Mission to Greece

I woke before dawn and ran to the top of Mount Olympus and struck the warrior's pose in yoga or the good morning pose, arms together overhead and in a forward standing split. A cock crowed, the moon was waning in the West and the sun waxing in the East. Below in the valley was Zeus' altar next to the ancient Olympic Games running track.

Here, I felt the vibration of the ancient Olympians thousands of years ago, and in hours, would be a part of Olympians from around the world witnessing the ritual of maidens with ancient togas chanting in ancient Greeks the very words these athletes heard before the Olympic games. The sun would then light the Olympic flame on Zeus' altar through a prism for the Los Angeles Olympics. It then would be run as a peace torch to light the flame for the 1984 LA Olympic games.

The day before, Guy Benjamin and I drove all day and arrived late in the afternoon. Olympia is at the top of Greece. I was to meet up with Elana Petchdakova, former wife of Valerie Brummel, the world record holder in the high jump whose form I watched in Tokyo in 1964. He approached the bar in long strides in a cat-like crouch low to the ground, then used his lead leg like a planted pole to catapult up over the bar. Americans went down, then up on the lead leg.

After seeing this, I learned how to high jump without practice. Elana was very close to John Thomas, and between the three of us, we promoted many US/USSR sports events in Moscow and in the US and founded Athletes United for Peace. The nuclear arms race was the shadow that propelled us to these peace efforts; we all felt the Cold War threatened humanity.

When Guy and I entered the great hall through a side door packed with Olympians, we saw Elana, deputy chairperson of the USSR Olympic Committee and gold medalist in the dressage, at the head table on stage. She saw me enter, leaped up, jumped off the stage, ran to me, and embraced me in one of the warmest hugs of my life. The athletes in the hall saw this and jumped to their feet in unison over the site of two Olympians from hostile countries in solidarity over peace.

Ancient Olympians from Athens and Sparta became friends through competition at the Olympic Games. According to tradition, the Olympic Torch or Ekekheiria (the sacred truce) calls upon all states to stop hostilities and mutual destruction on the battlefield, as well as the threat of violence. When lit, Ekekheiria signaled the cessation of wars and peace so that the Olympic Games participants could travel to the games safely and, during the games, could compete in peace and safety.

Zeus' altar was just yards above the running track. After being lit by the sun, the torch was to be transported to the length of Greece on its way to Los Angeles. I was asked to present petitions signed by hundreds of individuals in Greece, as well as trade unions and cultural organizations protesting the LA Olympic Committee's selling of the Olympic Torch for money. If you paid the fee, you could carry the torch, but the Greek people thought this was a violation of the spirit of the ancient Olympic Games. The Greeks arranged a protest along the route to Athens.

The US Olympic Committee, understanding this protest would be bad for public relations, then decided to fly the torch out of Olympia by helicopter. They lit the torch next to the helicopter with a cigarette lighter and abandoned the authentic torch; it was a bastard torch and not the real Olympic Torch. Jeff Fishman, a fraternity brother of Peter Ueberroth, headed up this hair-brained idea, and it was my mission to hand him the petitions.

I called the LA Olympic Committee and found Fishman's phone and address but got no answer, so I was stonewalled. Time was getting short. So, I drove to Washington DC and asked my Tokyo opening ceremony marching fellow Olympian, Senator Bill Bradley, fellow Southern California Striders senior runner, now US Senator Alan Cranston, like Bradley and Paul Tsongas, another Senator, to sign a letter of introduction for me requesting a meeting with Fishman on the torch run. I received no answer!

On the day of the public announcement in New York of the start of the Olympic games, I went to the hotel near the grandstands set up for the ceremony. I sat in a chair in the lobby, contemplating what a failure I was to the Greek people.

I had the petitions in my lap, so I closed my eyes and just meditated on what to do. When I opened my eyes, just two feet from my chair before me was Tom Bradley, Mayor of Los Angeles, Peter Ueberroth, USOC head of the Olympics, and a top woman from the International Olympic Committee.

I stood up and turned to Tom Bradley, introduced myself, and said, "I read your speech before the Winter Placid Olympics, and I was hoping that today you would deliver the same message of peace."

He looked at me with a dazed stare, and he knew my name. I turned to Ueberroth and introduced myself. Before I could say anything, he said, "Some of my staff are members of Athletes United for Peace."

I gave my spiel about Ekekheiria and the Olympic Torch, and I was asked to present these signatures and a proclamation. I extended my hand with the petition, and his hands went to his side. He motioned for an assistant to accept the papers. An assistant waiseved for all of us to proceed to the grandstands. I went with them, and halfway across the street, I envisioned a scene by security to oust me. I did not want this humiliation. I had done my duty. I pivoted around.

Just days before, Ronald Reagan publicly announced that he could not guarantee the protection or safety of USSR athletes. Not only had the US Olympic Committee violated the Olympic Torch, but the president of the US also violated its philosophy: to protect athletes during the Games. Reagan had unleashed the right-wing reactionaries through his Cold War talk, who had taken violent actions in LA. My dream of the world coming together in peace was now a phantom!

In 1980, after years of helping to get China into the Olympics, Carter boycotted Moscow. Now, after years of organizing US/USSR events for friendship and peace with Elana and Thomas, things seemed to be falling apart. I retreated to the parking garage below the hotel and watched a small TV in the corner.

A bulletin came across that the USSR would not be coming to the LA Olympics. I called Elana in Moscow. She said that the Soviet athletes came together because they knew of my failure to contact the US Olympic Committee over the peace torch and also Reagan's announcement of no protection and the general Cold War hostility by Warhawks now in power.

The 1972 Munich Massacre was on all of our minds. She said they voted not to come, and this was not a decision made by the Soviet Olympic Committee but by athletes. Eight years of peace work down the drain. It seemed to me I had been fired at Rutgers as an ideological dissident, had no job, and the world was splintered apart, and the production of nuclear weapons went unabated.

Chapter 32: Getting the World Record

I had become familiar with night dreams of not finding the entrance to the Olympic stadium, searching all night for the right door, and they finally stopped after 58 years. Finally, my world record was recognized! I knew I had a good chance when the judge for the Court of Arbitration of Sport became Hon. Hugh L. Fraser, Judge (ret.), Ottawa, Canada, a Black sprinter for Canada.

The stars aligned because now athletes were in charge: John Chaplin, a star sprinter (getting the American record), then Lord Coe, a star distance runner, head of World Athletics (world record), sending my petition to CAS.

Now, the judges were all real athletes, brothers! Athletes who compete at a high level know the problems of injuries, bad weather, defeats, changes of public adulation, and family matters. Arthur Ashe, Muhammad Ali, Grant Birkinshaw, a star New Zealand long jumper, and recently Novak Djokovic, a star tennis player, all resonated with me because of this rarified space. Each drifted to me as someone with like experiences. This happened again in Eugene.

So, why these new dreams? If I were getting the world record, now scheduled in for Steve Prefontaine Stadium in Eugene, Oregon, did Seb Coe take it seriously when I threatened him that I would get the ghost Prefontaine to spook the Lord?

I thought it was a joke, but upon further thought, I had experienced those who I was close to visiting me after they died. These dreams were different. Where did they come from? Finally, I ferreted this out. Everything went wrong in Tokyo in 1964: the bus went without me to the stadium, and I was assigned to a long jump pit which had a warm-up area only 6' 2" tall, and I am 6' 4".

I could not run or sprint in the warm-up area because of the rain storm outside, and then not being able to measure my steps or run through my steps. Plus, the sole jumper in an Olympic competition who had the wind violently changing direction when I jumped. This, I figured, was the cause of the unsettled dreams that had gone on for days before I received justice in Eugene. Nature has to cooperate!

Lord Coe asked Mike Powell and Willie Banks to be my chaperons for the days in Eugene. Banks trained at UCLA, my training spot in LA, and I knew him well. Powell and I connected years before as he was training for the Olympic games. I was 60 at the time and showed him I could dunk the ball with one step.

He remembered that he was buffed with weightlifting and was now in great shape. He said he remembered me being in great shape, which he aspired to be and was. They both took it seriously, escorting me everywhere I went, and we all walked together. My son Kent, granddaughter Heaven, and daughter Quincey also joined the ensemble.

We were quite a scene: Kent, star Texas Rugby player; Heaven, a sprinter from WSU; Quincey, Hall of Fame at Portland State national champions volleyball, two world record holders in the long jump and triple jump; and Donna de Varona, gold medalist swimmer and family friend plus Tracy Sundlun, manager of the Olympic team. The talk never stopped. All abuzz! Watching the meet together, Powell and Banks sat to each side, others down the row.

What did we talk about? Injuries and defeats, getting taken down, and suffering humiliation with injuries and other injustices. One long session of memories that only we would be interested in. Powell was not able to defeat Carl Lewis until the Tokyo meet, during which he set the WR and beat Carl at his best, figuring out what it took mentally to do this.

Banks had seriously injured his hip early in his career and had a long period of recovery not understood by most. Many stories, and I had mine, seemed unending. Who would understand or even be interested? Yet, here I was with bad dreams before the big occasion. Was I nuts? What was going on?

The hour came near, and we all lined up in the hall to the stadium, ready to go. I finally had my due: national television, prime time, I would be honored like never before. Finally, about ten minutes before we got the word, the ceremony was canceled and delayed for 4–5 hours, out of prime time TV. The temperature was 115 degrees. Highest ever recorded! A javelin thrower had to lie down on the grass between throws because it was too hot. Her mother complained, so they delayed the competition. My dreams were prescient.

At 8 or 9 that night, they had the ceremony while the US Olympic trials' long jump had started. No national coverage. Based on the competitive marks I would have earned during that competition, I would have made the US Olympic team almost 60 years later. This was the golden lining of that day. The ceremony was short, and earlier, I sensed that the announcer had no interest in me, so I wrote their script and then sent it to them. When they announced the ceremony, my words spoke out.

Doctor Phillip Shinnick, NCAA All-American, US Olympic team, Captain of the US national team to the Pan Conference in Tokyo (1969), founder of Athletes United for Peace, and now, after 58 years, WORLD RECORD HOLDER. Short and sweet!

Eric Johnson from Seattle KOMO television years before, when I was advancing my world record, did a short interview with me. He paid personally and found the actual copy of my world record jump. He wanted a follow-up, so I then flew to Seattle for the interview at Husky Stadium. It went well because I had a personal connection with him. That interview received an Emmy, and then Edward R. Murrow won Best Sports Story of 2021.

Reflecting upon all that I have written and all the struggles to become the best in the world, I think most about what I heard about my world record effort was what the national news said that day: "Phil Shinnick was robbed of a world record by official negligence."

The upshot of this is that I was the tough-luck kid. Or, "I heard you set the world record, but the runway was downhill, or too much wind, or no wind reading, so no record."

As a scientist, I heard from officials that they would only accept direct evidence or an altimeter reading. In the case of accurate science, a measurement by an instrument is indirect. Since the instrument is manmade and reflects what the inventor wants it to do, it is limited in perception.

Reading the instrument requires human perception, so it is not direct observation. Human perception is direct observation. Sport, by its very limitations, does not believe in the truth of performance or indirect observation. If you make a jump shot and your foot is over the line, it is not good, even though the ball went through the net. It negates reality!

In tennis, if the ball lands over the line but makes it over the net, it does not count. This is based upon rules. In my case, there were not enough wind gauges to measure the wind for events that were happening at the same time. Human observation and other wind readings confirmed my legal jump, but this is not allowed.

I did not like to be defined in this way, the tough-luck kid. This had a bad effect on my own sense of worth; instead of being honored for a terrific effort, I was dishonored for 58 years. The only refuge was to go deep inside to stabilize my sense of worth and believe in truth.

Since these responses did not reflect the actual event as I experienced it, injustice was dealt to me by the outside world. It took all of my feelings of self-worth to overcome this. I could not be defined by the outside world or succumb like Ajax, the Greek warrior, who did not get honor for his braveness and went insane and killed himself. I am not alone!

Women have suffered this same way from misogyny, Blacks from racism, others intolerant of religious beliefs, or school bullying; all require a struggle for self-worth.

"Phil, if you know what you did, this is enough for you to know the truth."

This minimizes the effect the outside world has on the human psyche. Besides truth being honored and dishonor being negated in my long struggle with backward sports officials to get my world record, the process of competing itself is daunting.

This aspect of truth is a small part of being the best in the world and an Olympian. Competing at this level requires training to be the fastest, most powerful, and constant effort over many years. My efforts in training I would not put anyone else through, but I never accepted this or liked it.

My biggest injury came from attempting a world record. In practice, I could not imitate at that high level; it only could come in high-level competition. In the Cow Palace in 1963, I knew I was going to break the indoor world record, but three steps from the take-off, my hamstring cramped and pulled violently. It took five years to get my full speed back, but 8 months later, I made the Olympic team.

In 1972, at the US nationals, I cramped and pulled in in mid-flight for my best jump ever. My career ended with that. People do not like excuses and do not like to hear about pain and suffering, so I learned not to share this with anyone. Again, people expected world records, but if I tried at that level, I could hurt myself. I competed at a national level and was seen as a flash in the pan. I knew what people thought but could not do all-out jumping.

Trying to make the Olympic team loomed over my mind, never leaving me. If I had not made the team and yet broken the world record, more disgrace would have awaited me. I never slept deeply at night, thinking that if I let go and rested, I would be lost and not find the way.

Still, to this day, I sleep several hours, wake up, and meditate in the early hours. Night and day seem the same to me, just dark and light. My fate or consciousness never left me; I had to hold on.

When I got the WR, my nightmares stopped, which before came almost every night. I could not find the door to the Olympic competition, over and over again. The path to greatness means injury, mental stress, defeat, and dishonor. I fully accept this life and do not regret my competitive years or even to this day the long struggle. This is who I am!

I was honored for my high jumping, sprinting, and decathlon, which won me medals as a way to overcome my disgust with the long jump world record I set and the public response. I wanted to show I was a great athlete in all events. This story is half true; nature has something to say. I was all prepared to set a new Olympic record and win the gold medal at the Tokyo Olympics.

A rainstorm greeted me with shifting winds, but it was only for me. There was a muddy runway, and officials were thwarting my run-through and not qualifying. Another disgrace! I was given a reprieve at Modesto during my world record; the Sun and Moon aligned right, the wind died, full crowd and the best in the world there. Never again! These are forces in the world that must cooperate. They may happen or not, but they are beyond my control. It took me years to understand that my competitors and my training were not the issues.

Nature is a part of me through natural creation, and in a way, I do not fully understand this link, but I can say that on the outside, nature graced me and disgraced me. It is not concerned about honor or dishonor. I fully understand this, and for my part, I will not give up on honor or dishonor because it is a public cultural thing with roots back 3,000 years to the ancient Olympics. This ordeal led me to find worth deep inside me, and there, I found my true nature.

My time during my graduate studies at Berkeley taught me that journalists are the key to cultural change. So, I built relations with all the top outlets, *Sports Illustrated*, the *New York Times*, *UPS*, *West Coast Papers*, and magazines, and published in them or got others to write about the injustice of my world record and other sports and peace issues. I would not get the world record until the public sensibility changed and the people became sympathetic. This took years, and I felt humiliated, as if I came with a tin cup in my hand begging.

Yet, I had to do this for my own soul, to fight injustice and change the rules of sport at all levels, for my case and other issues as well. I have also worked for world peace and normalized relations with China and Russia over the last 40 years. Do sport, not war, as we are one people, and sports unite us!

Made in United States
Troutdale, OR
05/03/2024

19608655R00149